YOUR KNOWLEDGE HAS VALUE

- We will publish your bachelor's and master's thesis, essays and papers

- Your own eBook and book - sold worldwide in all relevant shops

- Earn money with each sale

Upload your text at www.GRIN.com
and publish for free

Bibliographic information published by the German National Library:

The German National Library lists this publication in the National Bibliography; detailed bibliographic data are available on the Internet at http://dnb.dnb.de .

Imprint:

Copyright © 2016 GRIN Verlag, Open Publishing GmbH
Print and binding: Books on Demand GmbH, Norderstedt Germany
ISBN: 9783668219861

This book at GRIN:

http://www.grin.com/en/e-book/322492/unleashing-volte-capabilities-assessing-the-migration-from-cs-voice-to

Omar Amoretti

Unleashing VoLTE capabilities. Assessing the Migration from CS Voice to IMS-based Voice over LTE (VoLTE)

GRIN Publishing

GRIN - Your knowledge has value

Since its foundation in 1998, GRIN has specialized in publishing academic texts by students, college teachers and other academics as e-book and printed book. The website www.grin.com is an ideal platform for presenting term papers, final papers, scientific essays, dissertations and specialist books.

Visit us on the internet:

http://www.grin.com/

http://www.facebook.com/grincom

http://www.twitter.com/grin_com

Master thesis

Unleashing VoLTE capabilities
Assessing the Migration from CS Voice to IMS-based Voice over LTE (VoLTE)

By: Mag. Omar AMORETTI, MSc

Vienna, 2016

Abstract

Operator-provided voice services will gradually migrate from today's circuit-switched (CS) voice networks to packet-switched IP networks, using Voice over LTE (VoLTE) as the foundation to provide telecom-grade telephony services. This paper presents the first implications of introducing IMS-based VoLTE in Germany, Austria and Switzerland (DACH) from a mobile operator's perspective. Further VoLTE performance aspects such as parameter optimization and HD voice are discussed, thus serving as a basis to then analyze the DACH mobile network test results for 2014 in terms of telephony and data performance. Overall results for a DACH VoLTE trial conducted in the third quarter 2014 complement the analysis.

Keywords: VoLTE, IMS-based VoLTE, HD voice with VoLTE

Table of Contents

1 Introduction

The increasing gap among capacity and demand poses an urgent call for novel network technologies to allow mobile operators to improve performance on a cost-effective basis. In fact, Voice over Long Term Evolution (VoLTE) is a key component for an innovative set of services determined for all-IP networks: the goal relies on making these novel applications as available as voice and messaging are nowadays, while also offering a flexible interaction with Internet applications.

Indeed, LTE focus on a (rather flat) all-IP access technology aiming at delivering a bandwidth-efficient approach for carrying several types of subscriber traffic at the same time. In other words, the capability of transporting Voice over IP (VoIP) services along with the provision of high-rate data throughputs, characterizes one of the critical drivers for the development to LTE. As of December 2014, six countries have deployed VoLTE[1] services and still 56 others are currently preparing its implementation [30].

VoLTE denotes a GSMA standards' profile for the provision of applications offered nowadays through Circuit Switched (CS) networks over the Packet Switched (PS) network of LTE. For many operators, VoLTE embodies a future-proof approach to rich media services, thus leaving no other reasonable alternative than to opt for its swift implementation. In this sense, the VoLTE deployment has underlined the importance of realizing the IP Multimedia Subsystem (IMS) and its related Session Initiation Protocol (SIP) within a wireless setting. Certainly, IMS and SIP are crucial in enabling VoIP services like VoLTE in a LTE environment.

---

[1] Additionally, 125 mobile network operators (MNO) in 77 countries have commercially deployed HD voice services by the end of the first quarter 2015 [30]

For instance, IMS delivers the gateway functionality and interconnection supporting the communication between VoIP and non-VoIP devices[2]. For its part, SIP determines the required signaling for authentication, call establishment and the delivery of complementary services[3]. Undeniably, to deliver 'telecom-grade' voice services (at least better than the legacy CS ones) is of outstanding relevance to VoLTE. In this regard, the VoIP implementation in a LTE setting clearly requires both technologies (SIP/IMS) along with LTE radio access network (RAN) features, which altogether enable VoLTE to outperform over-the-top (OTT) voice services [28].

Generally speaking, these OTT applications involve the provision of media (audio/video) to a subscriber's handset and rely on the specific Internet service provider (ISP) only as a carrier of bits and bytes. Definitely, OTT denotes not only streaming services[4], it also comprises VoIP speech applications.

Within this context, VoLTE[5] is predestined to turn into the key technology for IP-based communications. What is more, VoLTE enables even better high definition (HD) voice quality, bringing forward the mobile network operator's (MNO) competitive capabilities with regard to OTT VoIP providers. In the same manner, the MNO's strategy for voice as well as spectrum availability will ultimately shape the VoLTE's deployment. As operators define their implementation plans, the Circuit Switched Fallback (CSFB) might represent a first evolutionary approach, followed by the Single Radio Voice Call Continuity (SRVCC) as soon as VoLTE is launched[6] [35]. Alternatively, other MNOs would await eagerly for ubiquitous LTE coverage before their VoLTE service offering. In fact, the MNO's options will be affected by specific business goals, its technology architecture as well as strategic competences.

Rich Communications Services (RCS) will (analogous to VoLTE) benefit from IMS control capabilities, thus embracing an enriched multimedia portfolio. For instance, starting with the first VoLTE launch in 2012 in South Korea, a comprehensive variety of VoLTE-capable devices has been developed, leading many operators to launch it during 2014 (Asia and North America [30].

---

[2] non-wireless devices also included
[3] e.g. call retention or three-way calling
[4] Hulu, WhatsApp, Netflix, etc.
[5] together with a complementary conversational video service defined by GSMA
[6] prior to ubiquitous LTE coverage

Furthermore, the numerical data throughout presented in this document uses a comma ","
as decimal mark. Moreover, this paper is divided in four parts, the first of which describes
some key implications of the migration to IMS-based VoLTE (chapter two). Undeniably,
deploying VoLTE requires a number of optimization steps to gain the full benefit of the
technology's potential. This parameter optimization is the focus of chapter three. The fourth
chapter presents a high level analysis of two mobile network tests published in 2014 that
builds the basis for further findings regarding telephony and data (access) performance.
Particularly, this sheds light not only on the voice test methodology, but also on the
importance of VoLTE Friendly User Tests to better align the operator's voice capabilities
(over LTE) with the demanding user's expectations. Finally, some conclusions are drawn
based on the relevant aspects discussed, outlining the upcoming challenges operators will
cope with in the near term.

2 Migrating to IMS-based VoLTE: Initial considerations

The need for bandwidth derived from devices and subscribers has been constantly increasing for many years. Actually, the data volume transferred by mobile networks is doubling approximately every year and the quantity of connected machine-to-machine (M2M) devices is estimated to exceed 50 billion by 2020 [25]. Nevertheless, the compound annual growth rate (CAGR) is expected to decline in the years to come, from 4% per annum for 2008 – 2014 to a moderate 3,1% p.a. till 2020 [30].

In this sense, to take advantage of mobile-broadband opportunities (while at the same time increasing benefits for business and end-users) remains the focus of every operator's activities. LTE networks, for their part, are able to carry mobile broadband with huge data capacity and a minor latency level. Though, since there is no circuit-switched voice domain in LTE (Fig. 1), a universally interoperable IP-based voice and video calling solution for LTE is being implemented within the telecom industry: VoLTE [29] and ViLTE[7], which further facilitate the evolution of innovative communication services.

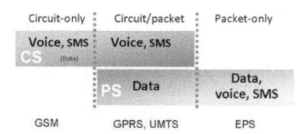

Figure 1: Circuit and packet domains. LTE within the Evolved Packet System (EPS) [1]

Furthermore, over-the-top (OTT) communication solutions like Skype (and most recently WhatsApp) have influenced the way users assess a particular service based on VoIP. According to an estimation [26] [30], the business loss derived from users using OTT voice services will amount to USD 386 billion for the period 2012 - 2018. Nonetheless, a completely satisfactory user experience cannot be offered by OTT solutions due to missing QoS measures or the lack of handover mechanisms to the circuit-switched (CS) network.

---

[7] A conversational video application founded on the IP Multimedia Subsystem (IMS) and defined by GSMA IR.94 [29]

In addition, there is no guaranteed emergency call support or extensive interoperability of services among diverse OTT services. Thus, the readiness of subscribers to use a service that does not offer security, quality, flexibility or even mobile-broadband coverage clearly influence the adoption of OTT services in a negative manner.

Furthermore, VoLTE is expected to be implemented together with CS voice, e.g. parallel to the ongoing evolution towards IMS-based VoLTE: its timing becomes vital for operators to prevent losing out to OTT providers and make the most out of VoLTE capabilities. Operators, therefore, apply the following methods:

- Spectrum refarming[8] allows to considerably limit the implementation expenses and supports twice as many calls within the same spectrum (e.g. spectral efficiency).
- Deployment expenditures can be substantially decreased in contrast to spectrum acquisition
- Network and planning optimization poses a cost restriction and facilitates future-proof network modernization

The past two years have seen a wave of LTE network deployments around the world [30]. Interestingly, most mobile network operators (MNO) still use a CS system because of their reliability in carrying voice services and also because of user preferences (many still use CS terminals). For instance, many MNOs are currently evaluating a suitable path to 'align' their networks with the Internet by migrating the entire services to a (LTE IP) packet-switched environment. For this purpose, the IP Multimedia Subsystem (IMS, [12]), a system standardized by the 3rd Generation Partnership Project (3GPP), has proven to be the commonly chosen solution.

---

[8] It can be considered as a process involving any basic change in the terms of frequency usage for a specific part of the radio spectrum

The clear advantage for IMS is its cost-effectiveness when shifting core telecom services (voice, video and messaging) to an IP environment. Additionally, IMS is more network-efficient than current systems and generates supplementary prospects for innovation in the medium term. Particularly, the basic IMS capabilities[9] can be reused by further services, thus rendering IMS a trend-setting and comprehensive solution in regard to a broader IP-communication approach. Besides, IMS is 'access-agnostic', meaning the support for seamless handovers and its independence of the connection method.

Regulatory measures

In general terms, the European Union follows a consumer-oriented as well as interventionist style. In fact, the drop of termination rates, e.g. the fees that one MNO charges another one for terminating calls on its network, has brought a significant weakening of the MNO's interconnection earnings. In this sense, the European Commission adopted by the end of 2013 a Recommendation [23] to the national regulatory authorities regarding the non-discriminative practices on costing methodologies in order to encourage competition and boost the investment in broadband infrastructure. Still, the European Commission proposed in the same year an EU Regulation targeted at the further development of the single market for electronic communications.

Furthermore, the EU strives to eradicate the roaming fees[10] for consumers within Europe. The 'Digital Single Market Proposal', presented by the European Commission two years ago, would involve a decline in roaming fees for messages, data and calls to the particular domestic termination rates level ('roam like at home') [23]. Irrespective of the proposal's result, this sort of harmonization is projected to happen in the medium term, causing returns to further deteriorate.

Moreover, competition authorities impose rigorous controls on telecom players with the aim of guaranteeing the (MNO) compliance with industry specific regulations. It is, therefore, indispensable that European network operators mitigate the negative profit effects owing to price-oriented competition and regulation by concentrating on profitable innovations and (market) sectors. Undoubtedly, finding the appropriate equilibrium among (infrastructure) capital expenditures and cost-efficiency is a crucial element to gain and maintain momentum.

---

[9] authentication, authorization, charging and routing
[10] a plan currently under discussion

Undeniable, a well thought-out (European Union's) regulatory method can fully benefit of the socio-economic impact derived from the mobile business by facilitating innovation in mobile connectivity and applications. So, the prospect of a 'connected' Europe is better accomplished by promoting investments as well as end-user confidence in novel mobile technologies.

2.1 Benefits of IMS-based VoLTE

In the medium term, VoLTE operators have a sustainable competitive positioning: they can deliver superior HD voice, implement video/messaging as well as converge with the web via Web Real Time Communications (WebRTC). Moreover, (VoLTE) operators can work in partnership with application providers and supply the best user experience on a low cost basis, because they can translate application developers' solutions onto innovative communication services. Also, a quick customization of features for strategic activities (as the mobile healthcare industry could be) becomes feasible and effective.

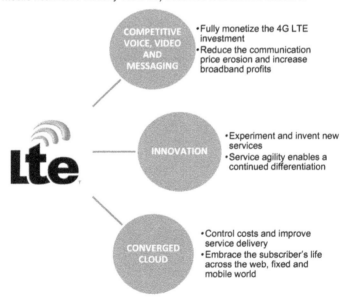

Figure 2: VoLTE's strategic value for operators. Adapted from [14]

Needless to say, VoLTE plays an important role in empowering all-IP communications in the 4G LTE network. As a result, VoLTE will enable operators to:

- Generate attractive communication services by merging mobile voice with video, the web and social networking
- Provide faster call setup times
- Improve customer experience by delivering data and better HD voice simultaneously (which also contributes to offload legacy infrastructure). In addition, the current 'fragmented' communications landscape that relies on various (rich) media approaches becomes more harmonized
- Migrate from dual radio CDMA (only in the USA) and LTE devices to LTE-only devices

Furthermore, the user value proposition for IP-communications[11] relies indeed in the MNO's traditional assets: while each service (RCS, VoLTE) delivers some real benefits compared to other approaches, the intrinsically user value proposition of IP-communications is not based on pioneering service enrichments, but rather on a superior user experience centered on reliability and interconnection as well (refer to Fig. 3).

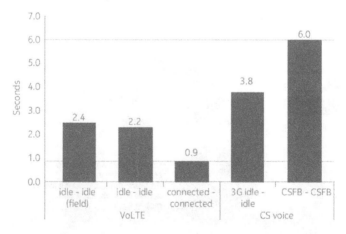

Figure 3: Call setup time measurements in comparison [36]

---

[11] which is comprised of VoLTE and IP-messaging or Rich Communication Services (RCS)

For sure, VoLTE is not the only method by which all operators will initially launch voice service in the short run. Yet, it embodies the ideal approach if competitive advantages and their related (business) risks are considered.

2.2 Providing voice over LTE

Despite the overwhelming enthusiasm on just exploiting LTE for data, several MNOs consider the provision of voice services as LTE is being implemented into the network. In an initial stage, some approaches involve the deployment of LTE to complement the already existent High Speed Packet Access HSPA/HSPA+ and EDGE coverage (within data-intensive areas for example). Additionally, the phased deployment of LTE throughout the whole network forces operators to safeguard the continuity of voice services (with slight service interruptions) as long as subscribers roam among 2G/3G and LTE networks. In the end, since that there is no other well-specified, wide accepted or well-supported solution, operators will have no other choice than adopting VoLTE.

For its part, 3GPP provides two standards for voice service provision in 4G LTE [3] [5]:

- VoLTE: Here, the LTE network (and IMS) care for the delivery of voice calls
- Circuit Switched Fallback (CSFB): Given an established LTE connection, the User Equipment (UE) has to fall back to 2G/3G the moment a call origination/termination occurs

Particularly, the CS Fallback (CSFB) and the dual-radio methods on which CDMA operators rely (in some cases known as Simultaneous Voice-and-LTE, SVLTE) are convenient to the extent that current telephony services are reused. However, these are not indeed LTE solutions and, as a result, are not subject to suitable development. Likewise, OTT methods are attractive since they run over IP and support, on the one hand, richer experiences. On the other hand, important features like interoperability and 2G/3G integration/handover are

(with the OTT approach) definitely at stake (see Table 1).

	Subscriber's Service	VoLTE	CSFB	App Providers
Standards	Global interoperability, including regulatory	Yes	Yes	No
	End to End QoS	Yes	Yes	No
	Roam with local voice, not home-routed data	Yes	Yes	No
Multimedia	4G LTE data simultaneous with voice	Yes	No	Yes
	All-IP network enables video-communications, etc.	Yes	No	Yes
	Foundation for services innovation, WebRTC , etc.	Yes	No	Yes
Voice	Minimal voice call setup delay	Yes	No	Yes
	Evolved voice: HD, new features, WebRTC , etc.	Yes	No	Yes
	Graceful continuity to 2G/3G circuit voice	Yes	Yes	No

Table 1: VoLTE compared to other approaches for voice in LTE devices. Adapted from [16]

The development path towards VoLTE, as shown in Fig. 4[12], may follow different approaches: without a doubt, some operators will opt for a blend of CS voice and LTE data (on LTE devices). Sooner or later, more profitable prospects derived from enriched voice services for LTE smartphones will persuade most MNOs to fully adopt IMS-based VoLTE. By delivering voice and data over the same network at the same time, a superior customer experience can be accomplished.

It should be noted that the features influencing the migration alternatives (e.g. rollout, coverage as well as the implementation speed) are not only determined by the present mobile technology or market conditions, but ultimately by the available spectrum in a particular site.

---

[12] VoLGA is not included in the graph since the standards have yet been accepted by 3GPP. Hence, it is outdated

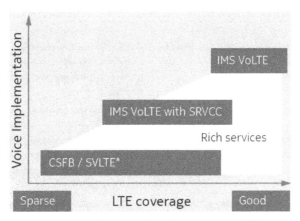

Figure 4: Voice Strategies: Providing voice over LTE [35]

2.2.1 Circuit-switched Fallback (CSFB)

CSFB embodies an initial stage in empowering LTE devices with the size, cost-effectiveness as well as power consumption benefits of single-radio approaches (in terms of 2G/3G voice combined with LTE data). In fact, CSFB reuses the legacy networks in order to deliver voice services for LTE. For this purpose, the handset[13] is required to fall back to the legacy network prior to the call setup origination/termination. In fact, CSFB provides feature transparency and a comprehensive service while facilitating operators to exploit their 2G/3G networks for the CS service provision.

---

[13] usually attached to the LTE network for data services

At first glance, some benefits and drawbacks derived from CSFB are outlined in Table 2

Benefits	Drawbacks
CSFB prolongs the lifecycle of 2G/3G networks by allowing them to support voice services for the LTE network	CSFB is fairly signaling-intensive and the time to complete the fallback (when both sides perform it) usually takes around 6 seconds (Fig. 3).
Many 2G/3G elements like CS service platforms, operations support systems (OSS), MSC, etc. are reused, thus guaranteeing a quick and reliable voice service rollout for LTE.	An extra call setup delay (due to the fallback) occurs when the handset performs measurements to locate an appropriate GSM/UMTS cell to use. Still, a location update is necessary before the origination of (or the reply to) a call.
For CSFB, no additional network components are required. Also, upgrades to current network nodes are rather minor versus other options	CSFB provides simultaneous voice and data on handovers to UMTS and GSM with Dual Transfer Mode (DTM). However, this is not the case when handing down to a 2G network lacking DTM: here, the PS session gets merely canceled.
CSFB modifications to the MSC are indeed simple since the SG interface was intentionally founded on the Gs interface (employed among the MSC and Serving GPRS Support Node).	Increased OPEX and risk: the economic and technical challenges that rise with the operation and maintenance of 4G LTE and legacy 2G/3G networks in parallel should not be underestimated.

Table 2: Assessing the CSFB approach

Nevertheless, operators who temporarily choose CSFB should critically reflect on the invested resources due to:

- Communication experience for end-users might be at stake: during voice calls CSFB subscribers would be downgraded from 4G LTE data service to 3G HSPA+ or 2G, losing data services completely.
- Boundaries are imposed on innovation: New services, which work on all-IP networks and are based on high quality video codecs, cannot be realized (such as video calling)
- In the medium term, CSFB has to be supported for devices lacking VoLTE capabilities and for inbound roaming subscribers

Another aspect to consider is the supply of devices via non-operator sales channels ('vanilla'[14] handsets), which may negatively affect the supported voice features. Even if carrier-controlled handsets will predominate, complex configuration steps would be necessary for those not provided by the MNOs.

2.2.2 Voice over LTE (VoLTE)

This approach relies on the IMS call control as stated by 3GPP TS 23.228 [12] for LTE voice application carriage. In fact, IMS delivers value-added innovative multimedia services by facilitating media additions and removals at whatever time throughout a call. Likewise, it is estimated that VoLTE will be extensively implemented in view of the wide-ranging LTE coverage, regardless of the visited network.

Furthermore, end-to-end IP real-time voice and rich media services are allowed by VoLTE executed with HSPA+ and LTE. Indeed, the benefit of this configuration is given by the seamless mobility among LTE and UMTS by means of packet-switched (PS) handovers/handbacks. For instance, VoLTE users would enjoy steady voice services independent of their attachment to a 2G/3G or LTE network. This is guaranteed by the IMS Centralized Services (ICS), in the case of 2G/3G CS service continuity, by linking the IMS call control to the GSM/UMTS access network. Despite these advantages, most operators do not follow the HSPA approach since it is less efficient for voice and QoS enforcement (e.g. delay).

Single Radio Voice Call Continuity (SRVCC)

Normally, a conversation would be dropped once the LTE signal get lost and no handover (towards 2G/3G) takes place. SRVCC and enhanced SRVCC[15] [2], standardized by the 3GPP, characterize in this context the VoLTE technology responsible for this handover as a way to guarantee the call continuity as soon as the end-user finds himself outside the LTE coverage. In other words, SRVCC stands for the call continuity among IMS (over PS/CS access) for conversations attached to IMS given that the handset is only capable of communicating on one of those access networks [17]. What is more, SRVCC performs network-controlled handovers, thus removing the necessity for the UE to connect to two access networks at the same time.

---

[14] e.g. without any (operator-side) customization
[15] This applies for international roaming. SRVCC is defined by the 3GPP standards TS 24.237 [7], TS 23.237 [5] and TS 23.216 [4]

From the abovementioned, the mobile device is not able to attach to more than one radio access networks simultaneously: this implies a cutting off from the LTE network and a reconnection to 2G/3G. Should this arise during a chat, the SRVCC determines the actions to be undertaken (e.g. SRVCC is not valid outside of a conversation). Another relevant factor is given by the IMS call control in the home network of the end-user, which implies that the (VoIP or CS-based) conversation is camped in the IMS domain.

Based on Fig. 5, the general SRVCC mechanism comprises an active VoLTE conversation represented by step 1, followed by a SRVCC handover (after abandoning LTE coverage): the Evolved Packet Core (EPC) 'talks' to the Mobile Switching Center (MSC), which initiates the transfer from LTE towards 2G/3G (step 2). Additionally, the MSC prompts the IMS to run a session handover, thus launching a new access route with the MSC. In the last third step, the IMS-controlled conversation is reinitiated over the CS core.

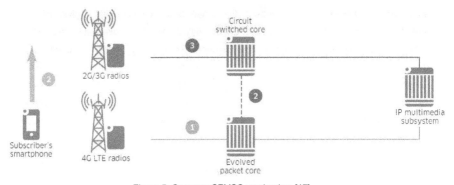

Figure 5: Common SRVCC mechanism [17]

Moreover, the SRVCC procedure implies not only a handset having a SRVCC client, but also requires the involvement of the Mobility Management Entity (MME), LTE's radio part, Service Centralization and Continuity Application Server (SCC-AS), the Home Subscriber Server (HSS) as well as SRVCC-upgraded MSCs). These components are further discussed in section 2.3.

IMS Centralized Services (ICS)

For the past years, IMS mobile telephony has been implemented as a response to the growing subscriber demands and the advent of novel 4G technologies. This is because IMS facilitates fast developing and comprehensive services above and beyond speech (video for example). Since LTE[16] is not yet available throughout the world, roaming for mobile IMS rollouts still embodies a challenge. Fortunately, 3GPP and GSMA have promptly react by outlining methods (e.g. IMS Centralized Services [15]) for the provision of worldwide accessibility of IMS-controlled speech applications[17]. Nevertheless, no general method has been defined, which implies an explicit mechanism for a particular network type.

The term service consistency (SC), in the ICS context, points out the access reliability of speech applications through 2G/3G and LTE networks. Particularly, SC comprises a wide range of calls, even those terminated/originated from an IMS subscriber for the duration of 2G/3G network coverage. For the sake of clarification, Fig. 6 illustrates the difference between SC (the field of ICS) and service continuity.

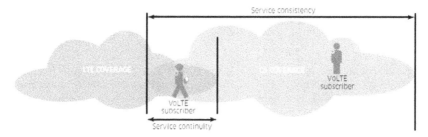

Figure 6: Service continuity compared to service consistency [15]

Furthermore, IMS-capable networks[18] (or those roaming to a capable one) enable IMS operators to offer separated (value-added) services to their subscribers. This may be defined as the home control pattern. However, many networks neither provide IMS VoIP (due to the absence of QoS controls) nor are IMS-capable, leaving one alternative for the provision of voice: the application of 2G/3G circuit-mode MSCs. In this case, a defined home-network pattern applies.

---

[16] employed to transport IMS
[17] even in CS networks
[18] An application server (AS) located in the home network performs service logic. Exceptions of the service logic apply for example for emergency services

To address the kind of incompatibility between the two settings (patterns), two options appear reasonable: the first one involves the selection of voice services that can be reliable provided via 2G/3G networks, while still offering superior speech applications through LTE. On the other hand, a set of features offering IMS home control to subscribers assisted by MSCs (3GPP ICS, [15]) may apply as the second alternative. Interestingly, most MNOs are opting for the first alternative as no reasonable method has been identified for the second one.

Table 3 examines further implications related to VoLTE

Benefits	Drawbacks
VoLTE empowers MNO to launch novel profit generating voice/data services (GSMA Rich Communication Suite for example). Service providers, from their part, are more tempted to provide converged fixed/mobile services on their wireless as well as wireline networks.	The adoption of ICS and SRVCC (in legacy networks) would call for the arrangement of a Media Gateway Control Function (MGCF) to support the Sv interface[19]. Similarly, improvements to each MSC contiguous to LTE/IMS networks might become indispensable
VoLTE make the most of the LTE/IMS network, bringing the operational cost reductions of relying on a flat IP network.	The LTE network demands a considerable investment owing to the introduction of the IMS core and the IP-SM-GW[20].
Simultaneous voice/data handovers (based on VoLTE realized with LTE/UMTS PS access) become feasible due to their management over a single PS domain.	Due to the complexity of the SRVCC signaling, a break in the voice stream may eventually be perceived by LTE subscribers (the case being a call 'handed-down' to the 2G/3G network). The enhanced SRVCC (eSRVCC, 3GPP Release 10) addresses this issue
Subscribers would experience equal voice services on the LTE or 2G/3G network in case of VoLTE deployed with ICS/SRVCC.	

Table 3: Assessing the VoLTE approach

---

[19] An upgrade of the HLR may prove indispensable to support the IP-SM-GW.

[20] IP Short Message Gateway. Besides, the HSS may need an upgrade for IP-SM-GW support as well

2.3 VoLTE Logical Architecture

2.3.1 4G LTE network architecture

The VoLTE application relies on the same modern communication network as is the case for the Rich Communications Suite (RCS), fixed broadband VoIP or messaging services (few exceptional features may apply to the LTE network[21]). As a consequence, VoLTE exploits the reliability of current commercial networks with regard to operations, performance, scaling, etc. What is more, this reliability strengthens the VoLTE's attraction since it leverages the service convergence across the web and mobile world. Some specific functions, which represent a service differentiation for the VoLTE operator, are also provided by VoLTE:

- Emergency calling
- Smooth handover of in-progress calls from VoLTE to CS
- Intelligent Network (IN) service migration
- QoS

Having this in mind, MNOs should exploit the VoLTE's (added) value by intensifying the partnerships with application providers. In fact, VoLTE is conceived to 'fit in' within the current subscriber's voice experience[22] by being transparent (whether the call is a VoLTE or CS one) and simply dependent on the attached radio access technology. As will be described later, novel wideband codecs may offer a superior voice quality and bring the user experience to the next level.

Furthermore, the 3GPP Release 8 builds the foundation for the VoLTE profile. Obviously, not all the functionalities stated by this release are necessary to guarantee VoLTE compliance (some features rely on higher releases). Particularly, the VoLTE logical architecture comprise:

- The **Radio Access Network (RAN)** is characterized by the Evolved Universal Terrestrial Radio Access Network (E-UTRAN[23])

---

[21] to guarantee QoS or handover voice calls from LTE to 2G/3G
[22] known from CS voice devices
[23] e.g. LTE. In fact, LTE radio capabilities for FDD/TDD LTE apply to VoLTE

- The **VoLTE UE** comprises the features allowing the EPC and LTE RAN accessibility (and this, in turn, mobile connectivity). Moreover, a VoLTE IMS application as well as a nested IMS stack are necessary when granting VoLTE services.

- The **IMS Core Network** delivers the service layer for the supply of Multimedia Telephony (MMTel).

- The Evolved Packet Core (EPC) represents the **Core Network**.

The VoLTE architecture[24] is depicted in Fig. 7: here, the blend of functional nodes into a given physical node application appears possible (e.g. PGW and SGW). In this case, these specific interfaces (S5 for example) become internal interfaces.

2.3.2 VoLTE Functional Node Description

The (VoLTE architecture's) relevant functional nodes as stated by 3GPP are explained in Fig. 7[25]. Further information regarding the VoLTE Service Description and Implementation Guidelines can be found in [31].

a) VoLTE User Equipment (UE)

This refers to the LTE capable equipment necessary to attach to the EPC, e.g. a UE using the LTE-Uu interface to connect to the EPC

b) Evolved Universal Terrestrial Access Network (E-UTRAN)

EUTRAN comprises a unique node linking with the UE: the eNodeB, which houses the Medium Access Control (MAC), Physical (PHY) and Radio Link Control (RLC)[26] layers. Moreover, the eNodeB is in charge of admission control, radio resource management, (de)compression packet headers (DL/UL) or the enforcement of agreed QoS.

---

[24] Interconnect and roaming are also included. In addition, the Gm (UE to P-CSCF) and Ut (UE to TAS) interfaces are built-in in the VoLTE architecture. This is, however, not depicted in Fig. 7.
[25] Further information available in 3GPP TS 23.002 [10]
[26] these incorporate the features of encryption and user-plane header compression

Table 4 provides further information on the other two components, the Evolved Packet Core (c) and IP Multimedia Subsystem (d). Particularly, IMS stands for the control structure empowering the upcoming generation of IP multimedia services. Some of the omitted IMS components[27] in Table 4 are thoroughly explained in [31].

---

[27] Interconnection Border Control Function/Transition Gateway (IBCF/TrGW), IMS-ALG/IMS-AGW (IMS Application Level Gateway/IMS Access Gateway), Media Resource Function (MRF), MGCF/IMS-MGW (Media Gateway Control Function / IMS Media Gateway)

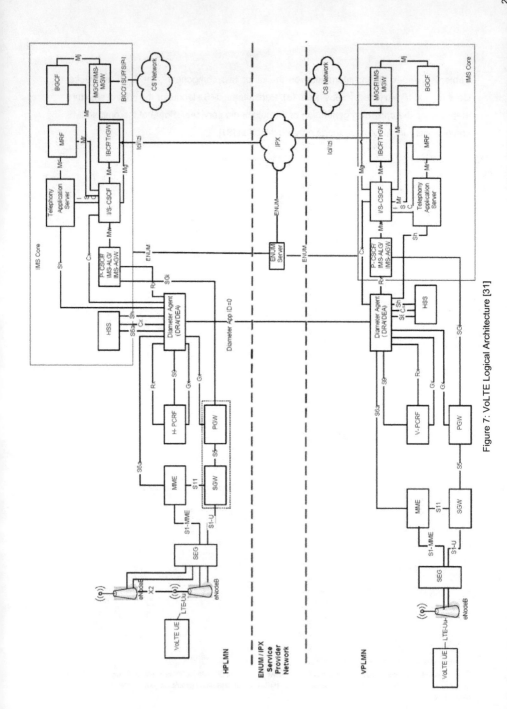

Figure 7: VoLTE Logical Architecture [31]

c) Evolved Packet Core (EPC)	d) IP Multimedia Subsystem (IMS)
Home Subscriber Server (HSS): Besides the storage of subscribers' dynamic and static information, the HSS delivers user profile data to the IMS core and MME while the IMS registration or UE attachment is performed.	**Telephony Application Server (TAS):** This is an IMS Application Server supporting a series of binding Multimedia Telephony (MMTel) services[28].
Serving Gateway (SGW): The SGW characterizes the local mobility anchor for inter-eNodeB handovers and inter-3GPP mobility[29]. Apart from packet forwarding and routing, the SGW replicates the user traffic given a legitimate interception.	**Proxy Call Session Control Function (P-CSCF):** The IMS-enabled VoLTE UE firstly contacts the P-CSCF for session signalling. By delivering SIP messages among the IMS Core Network and the UE, the P-CSCF performs the role of a SIP proxy. Furthermore, it maintains security links between the VoLTE UE and itself.
Policy Charging and Rules Function (PCRF): Basically, the PCRF cares for an appropriate user plane traffic handling in compliance with the subscriber's defined settings. Also, it is responsible for flow-based charging supervision as well as policy control arbitration. In this sense, the PCRF regulates the treatment for a service data flow when it comes to perform its enforcement role.	**Serving Call Session Control Function (S-CSCF):** The S-CSCF supervises and registers specific sessions intended for billing. It also performs session set-up/control, routing jobs as well as the role of a SIP registrar for VoLTE UE[30]. Additionally, the S-CSCF administers calls comprising the end-user and HSS after the successful registration.
Packet Data Network (PDN) Gateway: The connectivity among external PDNs (Internet, IMS) and the UE is ensured by the PDN Gateway (PGW): for instance, real-time connectivity to several PDNs may apply. The provision of a UE traffic entry/exit point as well as the packet screening/filtering, policy enforcement or charging support represent some tasks belonging to the PGW.	**Interrogating Call Session Control Function (I-CSCF):** For all links having a subscriber of the operator's network as destination, the I-CSCF has to be connected. In the course of the IMS registration, the I-CSCF queries the HSS to find the proper S-CSCF to handle the (registration) request[31].
Mobility Management Entity (MME): For the LTE access network, the MME characterizes its main control node: as such it cares along with the HSS for the user authentication and allows the UE to camp on the service provider's PMN. The MME deals also with the bearer (de)activation procedure and handles the generation/allocation of provisional identities to the UE. Likewise, the MME delivers the control plane functionality to enable mobility among 2G/3G and LTE access networks. Last but not least, it is accountable for selecting the Serving Gateway (throughout the initial attachment and intra-LTE handover) for the UE.	**BGCF (Breakout Gateway Control Function):** Defining the following hop for the conveyance of SIP messages, based on the routing setup information, is managed by the BGCF. There are, essentially, two termination events in (peer) IMS domains and CS ones: in the first case, the BGCF pick out the suitable Interconnection Border Control Function/Transition Gateway (IBCF) to manage the liaison to the peer IMS network. In the second case, the BGCF takes the proper MGCF based on expected CS domain breakout. **MGCF/IMS-MGW (Media Gateway Control Function / IMS Media Gateway):** This component is in charge of the control/media plane interworking[32], which also comprises CS networks founded on the Bearer Independent Call Control/ ISDN User Part (BICC/ISUP)

Table 4: VoLTE architecture: EPC and IMS components

28 Stated by 3GPP and outlined within the GSMA PRD IR.92 [29]. It involves supplementary service functionalities for example
29 by handing on the traffic to the PGW and 2G/3G
30 which the I-CSCF and HSS previously assigned to it
31 Upon call termination, the S-CSCF to which the subscriber is registered on is queried.
32 at the network interconnect point to CS domains

2.4 Assessing the Voice Quality Performance

Providing voice services over IP-based mobile networks requires not only telecom features (e.g. QoS) but also end-to-end proven network-to-device functionality. Definitely, voice represents an essential service and has, therefore, become a key distinguishing feature in view of the acute competition within the telecom industry. And it is here where High Definition (HD) voice[33] comes into play: based on wideband audio links, the human voice can be replicated more precisely, leading to an indeed natural sounding speech.

Certainly, traditional telephony is limited by traditional standards which results in subscribers perceiving a considerable quality enhancement with HD Voice. For instance, even the current digital telephony standards[34] are built on 1960s digital circuit technology and 1930s microphone know-how. G.711 was (prior to the introduction of HD voice) the voice quality standard, meaning that mobile telephony was able to provide less than this quality level.

Fig. 8 depicts the criteria determining the voice quality experienced: the handset cares for many of these parameters, others are however dependent on the network capabilities[35]. In fact, the voice quality among the PS (VoLTE enabled in LTE) and CS networks remains the same since an identical voice codec mode is applied. It is the delay parameter that makes the difference due to the substantial difficulty in managing it.

Particularly for PS services, delay stands for the crucial feature when it comes to attain an ideal balance in terms of voice quality versus voice capacity (mainly on the radio network). In this sense, the jitter buffer manager's performance becomes decisive in facilitating outstanding VoLTE services (Fig. 8) as a great amount of (packet delay) variations on the radio network have to be managed[36].

---

[33] codec G.722.2
[34] ITU-T G.711 Pulse Code Modulation (PCM)
[35] and others are present in the handset, but influenced by the network
[36] up to 80msec per link has to be handled according to 3GPP TS 23.203 [4]

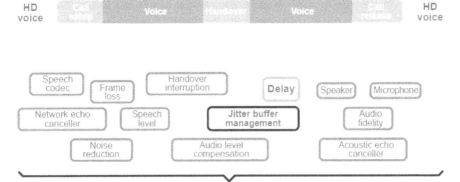

HD voice · · · Voice · · · Handover · · · Voice · · · · · · HD voice

Speech codec	Frame loss	Handover interruption	Delay	Speaker	Microphone
Network echo canceller	Speech level	Jitter buffer management			Audio fidelity
Noise reduction		Audio level compensation			Acoustic echo canceller

These are the same end-user requirements for VoLTE and 3G voice – the difference is that delay is distributed in another way end to end.

Figure 8: Parameters determining the user-perceived voice quality [28]

2.4.1 Leveraging the Operators' Assets

Operators should pay special attention to exploit the high quality potential telecom voice services are able to offer. In effect, carrier-grade VoIP services founded on VoLTE are at all times prioritized in the mobile network compared to other data traffic. Over the core and radio networks, QoS mechanisms are in place to care for key real-time services and their quality. Over-The-Top (OTT) VoIP services run, on the contrary, as best-effort[37] data over the mobile broadband access. And here is where the codecs for HD voice play an important role: they allow MNOs to employ them (e.g. codecs) with no major side-effects on the radio frequency (RF) capacity. Moreover, operators are able to combine a certain level of HD voice even when moving to 2G/3G. This efficiency advantage means that the new codec for HD VoLTE will neither demand any improvements of the VoLTE radio infrastructure nor additional RF capacity.

---

[37] e.g. no guarantee of good voice service quality for users

Global interoperability is also a relevant operator asset to build on. Indeed, the global E.164[38] community builds a distinctive entity for billions of phone users: to reach one person's handset, wherever in the world, through the phone number is a valuable asset that telephony service providers have built over the years. In this sense, operators can benefit of a lead position over OTT opponents by further delivering interoperable voice services. Still, advancing the voice quality experience even further, mainly based on interoperable HD voice enhancements, will unleash superior advantages to all stakeholders.

Beyond HD Voice

For users to experience HD voice via diverse IP-based voice applications, services are compelled to apply interoperable voice codecs. Many of them are, nevertheless, being developed throughout the market, further intensifying the voice services' fragmentation and rising transcoding expenses. As previously mentioned, the advantages of telecom-grade services might become obsolete if no interoperability is guaranteed. Nevertheless, VoLTE relies on the HD voice codec as its handset's default (AMR-NB, AMR-WB). What is more, some steps beyond HD voice have already been undertaken.

These efforts led to Evolved HD voice for LTE (EVS), which has been standardized in 3GPP and included in the profile IR.92 [29] and implies that HD voice services will offer a more natural voice quality in any sort of communication setting. This is accomplished by including a broader audio range for the perceptible frequency band as shown in Fig. 9.

Based on the IMS-based (3GPP) VoLTE, no additional components are necessary for EVS. In other words, those network elements having an integrated media handling functionality (e.g. SBG[39], BGF and MRF) may need an upgrade. For the case of VoLTE systems founded in IR.92 [29], just the addition of the EVS codec to the control plane would be required. From the subscriber's perspective, the UE has to fulfil some requirements (acoustics, processing capability, codec support) to fully enjoy EVS. Detailed information on this matter can be found in [24].

---

[38] E.164 represents an ITU-T recommendation defining a numbering plan for the worldwide public switched telephone network (PSTN) and a few other data networks

[39] Session Border Gateway (SBG), Border Gateway Function (BGF) and Media Resource Function (MRF)

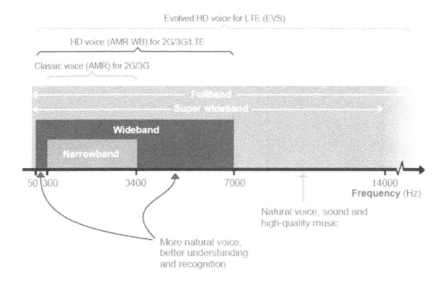

Figure 9: Audio bandwidths for mobile voice services. [24]

2.4.2 Development of audio testing

Mobile handsets and VoIP networks make use not only of codecs that considerably modify the (original) sound, but also apply limited bandwidth/bitrate. Regardless of these limitations, the perceived voice (quality) is still satisfactory as a result of the right tradeoff among various audio metrics such as the frequency response and a satisfactory speech perception.

For the purpose of voice quality measurement, the Perceptual Evaluation of Speech Quality (PESQ) was developed in the year 2000 and rapidly became an extensively applied tool. Its successor, POLQA (Perceptual Objective Listening Quality Assessment), additionally supports LTE, VoIP technologies, HD Voice, etc. Similar to PESQ, POLQA assessments are closely related to tests with human subjects.

POLQA[40] has been recognized as the modern Mean Opinion Score (MOS) benchmarking technology for mobile networks. The horizontal axis in Fig. 10 depicts the evolution of network technologies existing at the time of their development. A novel POLQA version was implemented in the third quarter 2014[41].

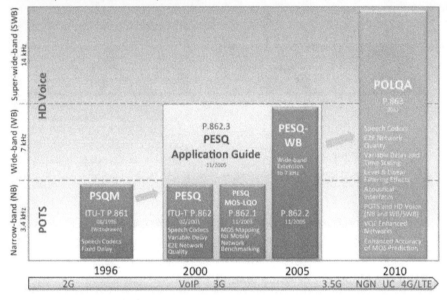

Figure 10: Evolution of ITU-T recommendations for voice quality testing [37]

POLQA and PESQ reproduce the expected (measurement) results of humans with actual speech samples, thus enabling speech-delivery system designers to guarantee a top subscribers' satisfaction level (refer to Table 5). Furthermore, POLQA is designed for these supplementary test tasks:

- Discontinuous Transmission (DTX), Comfort Noise Insertion
- Terminal testing: Analysis of the influence of the transducer during transmission/reception
- Voice Enhancement Devices (VED), Noise Reduction (NR)
- Voice Activity Detection (VAD), Automatic Gain Control (AGC)

---

[40] the third generation perceptual voice quality test method standardized as P.863 by the ITU-T in 2011
[41] The POLQA Coalition (OPTICOM, SwissQual and TNO) proposed an evolved version to ITU-T Study Group 12, which was approved as Rec. P.863 Edition 2.4 in 09/2014.

	PESQ	POLQA
Correct scoring with high background noise	No	Yes
Measurements with acoustic transducers	No	Yes
Effects of speech level in samples	No	Yes
AMR vs. EVRC codec comparison	No	Yes
Narrowband (300 Hz - 3400 Hz)	Yes	Yes
Wideband (100 Hz - 7000 Hz)	Yes	Yes
Super Wideband (50 Hz - 14000 Hz)	No	Yes
Linear Frequency distortion sensitivity	No	Yes

Table 5: PESQ versus POLQA. Adapted from [19]

2.4.3 PESQ/POLQA methodology

The audio quality of various (speech) samples was traditionally evaluated by several persons within the range 1 to 5 (5 being the best score). All weighted single scores generated then the Mean Opinion Score (MOS). However, such measurements relying on people were time consuming and costly.

To address this issue, tools that comprise algorithms relying on psychoacoustic patterns (e.g. PESQ, POLQA) can be applied. Ideally, these patterns would be consistent with the findings obtained from human groups. Indeed, this algorithm-based approach permits fast reiterations throughout the development process. Interestingly, the reproducible (measurement) results are regarded as unbiased since they are independent of any test condition or human behavior.

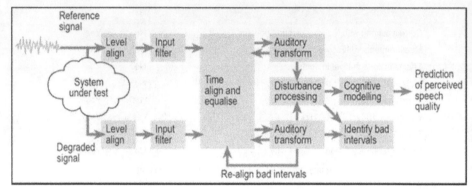

Figure 11: Perceptual audio test block diagram [19]

Fig. 11 depicts how perceptual audio examinations work: both signals, the degraded and the reference one, are independently level-aligned and screened with the receiving handset's transmission features. Moreover, both signals are time-aligned so as to balance minor time alterations arising from coding, delay or jitter. Next, a conversion from the time-amplitude into a frequency-loudness domain (e.g. auditory translation) takes place for the two aligned/filtered signals. This can be interpreted as the alterations noticeable by a human hearer.

In a later step, both signal representations are deducted from each other, yielding an estimation of the perceptible variations: these (variations) are then gathered over time and individually weighted based on various distortion sources[42]. Finally, the Mean Opinion Score (MOS) value is derived to label the voice quality (Table 6).

MOS	Quality	Impairment
5	Excellent	Imperceptible
4	Good	Perceptible but not annoying
3	Fair	Slightly annoying
2	Poor	Annoying
1	Bad	Very annoying

Table 6: MOS Score Summary

---

[42] e.g. subject to added distortions or if portions of the signals were absent after the broadcast (drop-outs).

3 VoLTE Parameter Optimization

Deploying VoLTE requires a number of optimization steps (in the radio and transport network) to gain the full benefit of the technology's potential. Ideally, the success rate and the retainability of a VoLTE call must exceed the level provided by CS connections.

Basically, network optimization involves the activation of features and optimization of parameters such as:

- Robust Header Compression reduces the bandwidth associated with the headers used to transport relatively small encoded audio packets
- Transmission Time Interval (TTI) Bundling overcomes the limitation of using short (1ms) TTIs at cell boundaries

These features contribute to make a VoLTE call reliable while still providing more efficiency compared to OTT VoIP applications. Special attention is paid, therefore, to decreasing the necessary bandwidth for voice and get the most out of the capacity. By doing so, the handover, setup and call completion success rates could be further improved.

In terms of handset power consumption, the focus lies on the one hand on the enhancement of the handset architecture: the integration of VoLTE into the chip set or the sleep mode available to the application processor fall into this category. On the other side, radio features like the Discontinuous reception (DRX) intended to conserve the UE's battery life during a VoLTE conversation complement the (handset) power saving solutions. Other valuable drivers are:

- Dedicated Bearers allow for the prioritization of VoLTE audio packets over all other best-effort traffic
- Semi-Persistent Scheduling (SPS) reduces the complexity and overhead of the continuous allocation of DL/UL physical layer resource blocks to transport the audio traffic

Additional (optimization) features in the field of speech quality, depending primarily on the voice codec sampling rate and the derived audio bandwidth, will be discussed separately.

3.1 Robust Header Compression (RoHC)

RoHC takes advantages of the redundancy of information present in

- the headers of subsequent packets in the same audio stream and
- various headers in different protocol layers

with the goal of decreasing the header size used to transport VoLTE audio. In fact, the 40-60 bytes of header length can be condensed to 3-4 bytes. And this applies to VoLTE calls, which usually comprise small encoded audio packets transmitted every 20ms.

Particularly, the size of the data is smaller than the headers for the protocols used to carry the encoded data. For VoLTE deployments based on IPv6, the mix of RTP/UDP/IP headers can sum up to 40-60 bytes long headers. This means that a VoLTE encoded audio transmission (relying on the Wideband-AMR[43] codec and RoHC) is reduced from 75 bytes to approximately 35 bytes.

As shown in Fig. 12, RoHC is used over the air interface to preserve the RAN's valuable bandwidth. In fact, RoHC may accomplish around 50% reduction in the size of VoLTE audio transmissions: the required bandwidth for any call is reduced while the amount of users on a given eNodeB site is increased.

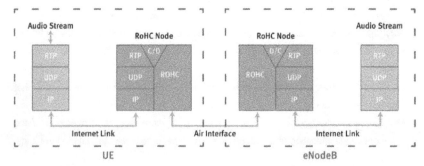

Figure 12: RoHC Compression and Decompression at the UE and eNodeB [44]

---

[43]   Adaptive Multi-Rate Wideband (AMR-WB) codec G.722.2

3.2 Transmission Time Interval (TTI) Bundling

LTE presents a shorter TTI (1ms subframe) than earlier defined in cellular technologies. In fact, a smaller TTI enables low over-the-air latency for real-time applications since resource scheduling is performed for every TTI. Some uplink issues are, though, caused by the short TTI in specific settings of an eNodeB's coverage: given an UE located at a cell edge (with deteriorating reception and no possibility of enhancing its transmission power), the eNodeB may activate the TTI bundling. In other words, the UE will intensify the error detection and correction related to each data broadcast by transmitting over several TTIs. Based on this improved approach (e.g. error detection/correction), overall latency is diminished compared to the use of a single TTI.

As presented in Fig. 13, TTI bundling contributes to lower-latency VoLTE data at cell edges, where information errors are predictable. Instead of waiting for the HARQ[44] process (typically 8ms/period) to send a data retransmission request, a data retransmission is assumed by TTI bundling: by doing so, several data packets are filled into a HARQ interlace period in advance. As a result, every packet comprises the identical source data coded with 4 distinct groups of error detection/correction bits.

Generally speaking, the short 1ms TTI (along with its bundling approach) represents for VoLTE a considerable advantage: it improves the uplink performance at cell edges by means of multiple bundled TTIs to transfer higher error detection and correction information.

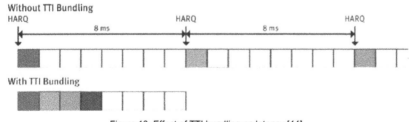

Figure 13: Effect of TTI bundling on latency [44]

---

[44] Hybrid Automatic Repeat Request

3.3 Discontinuous Reception (DRX)

For packet-based voice services, each encoded audio packet transmission (usually 20ms for VoLTE) is followed by a period of no transmission. DRX exploits, for instance, these silent periods by switching off several components such as digital signal processors, UE's RF receiver or A/D converters. As a result, the device's battery life can be conserved.

Nevertheless, setting a too long 'sleep period' might involve latency issues at the detriment of the wanted QCI value level (e.g. a predefined performance profile). Particularly, the network establishing the DRX pattern (and also being aware of the data downlink schedule to the UE) should carefully select a suitable DRX configuration in view of likely retransmission needs and latency constraints of the application. In this sense, special attention should be paid to the influence of TTI on DRX in LTE so as to improve DRX settings in favor of power saving.

As depicted in Fig. 14, the two DRX operation modes can be applied according to the pause duration within a chat: a long DRX deactivates the UE receiver for a longer time period in a situation where audio packets are not frequently delivered. The eNodeB's MAC Layer or an activity timer at the UE would regulate the transition from short to long DRX and vice versa. Worth mentioning is the absence of DRX short or long cycles in UMTS (only fixed-length ones are available).

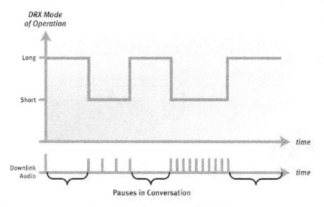

Figure 14: Long and Short DRX [44]

3.4 Dedicated Bearers

Despite the increased spectral efficiency offered by LTE, over-the-air bandwidth remains a limited and valuable resource. Moreover, Internet-based VoIP services usually generate a greater load on mobile networks, leading to negative (quality) side-effects. Operators need, therefore, to invest in more capacity to cope with the OTT voice traffic since (their) voice applications naturally consume additional network resources. In other words, each application along with the associated data strives for that finite bandwidth.

In fact, the encoded voice packets an off-the-shelf VoIP client produces do not show a significant difference when compared with data traffic derived from web browsing or video streaming (from a network's perspective). As a result, the network tries to bundle all users' (generic) data traffic into a single common channel[45]. Interestingly, with a default EPS Bearer no control over the service quality is possible. This implies a 'best effort' approach to transport all generic traffic to the Internet PDN. By the time the network resources are (temporarily) exhausted, latency may greatly fluctuate and packets be dropped due to data traffic queuing.

To overcome these drawbacks, which cannot be tolerated for real-time applications, LTE introduces the EPS Dedicated Bearer: It permits the isolation of certain types of data traffic (VoIP traffic versus FTP file download for instance). For VoLTE, an EPS dedicated Bearer will exclusively convey encoded voice packets among the UE and an IMS PDN-GW. Also, each Dedicated Bearer can possess diverse quality characteristics defining a QoS Class Identifier (QCI).

- Packet Delay Budget: The Maximum tolerable end-to-end delay among the UE and the PDN-GW
- Resource Type: Guaranteed Bit Rate (GBR) and Non-GBR
- Allocation Retention Priority: In case the capacity is depleted, scheduling is based on the value assigned ('1' equals to the highest level)
- Packet Error Loss Rate: Threshold level of IP packets not effectively received by the Packet Data Convergence Protocol (PDCP)

---

[45] e.g. the Physical Downlink and Physical Uplink Shared Channels PDSCH/PUSCH, having one or more EPS bearers linking the UE to the PDN-GW

Table 7 further presents standardized QCI values, '1' being assigned to VoLTE traffic that would be prioritized over all best-effort traffic on the Default Bearer.

QCI	Resource Type	Priority	Packet Delay Budget (ms)	Packet Error Loss Rate	Example Services
1	GBR	2	100	10^{-2}	Conversational Voice
2	GBR	4	150	10^{-3}	Conversational Video (live streaming)
3	GBR	5	300	10^{-6}	Non-conversational video (buffered streaming)
4	GBR	3	50	10^{-3}	Real-time gaming
5	Non- GBR	1	100	10^{-6}	IMS Signalling
6	Non- GBR	7	100	10^{-3}	Voice, video (live streaming), interactive gaming
7	Non- GBR	6	300	10^{-6}	Video (buffered streaming)
8	Non- GBR	8	300	10^{-6}	Video (buffered streaming)TCP-based
9	Non- GBR	9	300	10^{-6}	(email, www, FTP)

Table 7: Standardized QCI Values. Adapted from [44]

3.5 Semi-Persistent Scheduling (SPS)

As previously stated, the physical layer relies on common channels (PDSCH/PUSCH) to deliver the data contained in the logical bearers. A way to allocate these channels appears necessary to avoid several users (on an eNodeB) attempting to use identical resources at the same time. Specifically, a LTE carrier is split into several subcarriers within the frequency domain, whereas in the time domain every subcarrier is gathered into 0.5ms time slots.

A cluster of twelve subcarriers in one time slot is referred to as a Resource Block (RB) and is defined as the smallest portion of the LTE physical layer (resource) that can be placed to a UE (refer to Fig. 15). Moreover, VoLTE encounters a challenge when it comes to granting control channel overhead: as each downlink/uplink RB must be granted, the (control channel) overhead for the ongoing allocation of RBs becomes unmanageable.

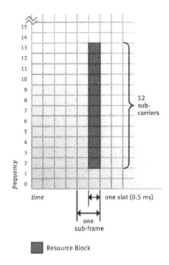

Figure 15: LTE Resource Block (RB) in the time and frequency domain (Physical Layer) [44]

To overcome this, Semi-Persistent Scheduling (SPS) was introduced to reduce granting overhead for applications such as VoLTE. In effect, the steady transmission configuration of VoLTE packets allows SPS to make a continuing grant of RBs instead of separately arranging each download/uplink RB. Of course, this involves a Radio Resource Control (RRC) message used to determine the RB grant's periodicity.

The green boxes in Fig. 16 illustrate the SPS-arranged RBs for a VoLTE call. As further shown by the orange box, additional RBs can be dynamically organized for data traffic while SPS is enabled (for example for a file download during a VoLTE call).

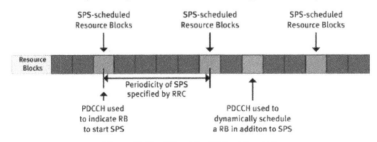

Figure 16: Semi-Persistent Scheduling [44]

Important to consider are the pauses (e.g. short-time silence periods) in the course of a VoLTE conversation: this may represent a drawback since (physical layer) resources get lost in case the SPS grant is continued. In this case, the expiration of the SPS grant after some network-defined transmission slots would be recommendable (uplink). In the end, it's all about finding the right balance between efficiency improvement (for shared data channels) and minimizing control channel overhead.

4 VoLTE Testing

4.1 Primary Implications

Table 8 depicts the relevant VoLTE testing areas and their related measures.

	Functional Aspects	Audio Quality	Performance Features
Goal	Verify parameters based on optimal settings	Signal analysis: Comparison of the reference signal with the one obtained	Assess the effect of fading, IP impairments and noise on audio quality. Note: different test settings for different test purposes
Measures	Check the LTE attach order	Audio quality assessment with proven approaches (e.g. PESQ/POLQA)	Analyze the UE capability to deal with IP traffic deficiencies
	Validate the IMS registration. Further test whether the UE is capable of registering to the IMS Server	Verify the UE audio quality for a VoLTE call	Assess the impact of fading on a VoLTE call sound quality
	Confirm that the Session Initiation Protocol (SIP) can launch a voice session	Acoustic signal assessment based on 3GPP TS 26.132 [4] Release 10	Test setup: CMW + UPV Audio analyzer + AMU
	Check if the UE is able to perform a VoLTE call	Test setup: artificial mouth and ear are required along with an audio isolated chamber	
	Examine the basic audio functionality through simple echo confirmation in loopback mode		

Table 8: VoLTE Testing Areas. Based on [39], [40]

Within the testing context, some key indicators have to be considered:

- **Accessibility**: It primarily assess the network access in order to get a service. A typical indicator would be a (network attach) failure ratio lower than 1%.

- **Retainability:** This term refers to the service capability to last (e.g. keep on providing the service) as long as this is requested by the subscriber. In terms of voice services, retainability sheds some light on network performance, especially when addressing the question how well can the network maintain calls (from the setup to their usual end). This data is vital in identifying poor performing cells, thus preserving the network against dropped calls. Here, a typical indicator is given by a dropped call ratio lower than 2%.

- **Integrity:** This indicates whether the network observed sound quality is regarded as 'good' in more than 95% of the total trials. A typical indicator of the speech quality would be characterized by 95% of all samples having a MOS better than 3.0.

4.1.1 Voice Quality of VoLTE versus OTT Voice Services

A voice quality evaluation of VoLTE and few others OTT voice services was conducted by Ericsson over commercial VoLTE-enabled LTE networks in South Korea [25] [28]. For this purpose, measurements were performed on two operator networks, employing three different first-class LTE smartphone brands: one of them was not available for VoLTE and another one was not permitted into one of the networks[46].

The tests were undertaken throughout the day and night (e.g. during low network load times). Moreover, a drive test was organized, generating around one hour of data per network, service and mobile handset. Also for the testing duration, a drive test application was linked to two identical handsets and the call nature was device-device. Furthermore, to reproduce the noticeable voice quality throughout a conversation, two factors needed were simultaneously examined: the speech path delay (SPD) as well as an estimation of the one-way audio quality (MOS-LQO$_{SWB}$[47]). Lastly, both parameters were depicted in parallel to evaluate the conversation's audio quality.

---

[46] Hence the number of measurements (e.g. the quantity of square-dots) in Fig. 17 varies among the services evaluated
[47] This represents the measurement unit used by POLQA on wideband speech

Fig. 17 illustrates the summarized outcomes of the obtained MOS-LQO$_{SWB}$ and SPD during the busy hours. In general, each square-dot[48] in the chart displays the 95th percentile SPD scores (e.g. 95% of the scores are better=lower) and 5th percentile MOS-LQO$_{SWB}$ results (meaning that 95% of the results are better=higher). Particularly, the dotted lines delimit a gray highlighted zone indicating common objectives for a first-class VoLTE service relying on both MOS-LQO$_{SWB}$ and SPD. Specifically, SPD will strive for less than 225ms and MOS-LQO$_{SWB}$ should achieve higher than 3.5.

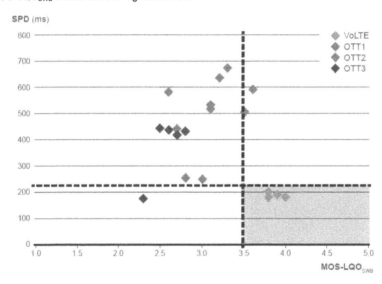

Figure 17: Voice quality results based on MOS-LQO$_{SWB}$ and SPD: VoLTE versus OTT voice services [28]

As seen in Fig. 17, VoLTE surpassed those (minimum) marks and none of the OTT voice services were even close. For VoLTE, the device as well as the network go through an explicit validation/integration procedure: the aim being the verification of the handset's jitter buffer and its ability to deal with major packet delay deviations, mainly near the (LTE network) cell border. On the contrary, a more volatile handset performance would be experienced with OTT voice services: not only because of the missing capability in handling (packet delay) variations, but also due to the missing QoS features.

---

[48] based on the measured combination of network and device

Generally speaking, all services may accomplish comparable MOS scores, but then again network priority is indispensable when a low SPD and hence an excellent voice quality is required. Additionally, handsets are explicitly devised for the provision of telephony services like VoLTE, since various standardization demands have to be met[49]. In a nutshell, VoLTE as a real-time telephony service is given priority over other services and handled via the MNO's network end-to-end[50]. This is, however, not the case for OTT VoIP services, which are combined with further data traffic and carried over the LTE network on a best-effort basis.

Performance of Combined Voice and Data services over LTE

Despite the fact that HD voice represents a differentiator for VoLTE subscribers, others factors such as the call setup time (CST) have to be considered as well: the CST can be enhanced to be as fast as one second, characterizing a major progress to the usual 4s goal in CS systems. Thanks to DRX, the handset is inactive for 'sleeping periods' during the packet delivery and reception, leading to a minor energy usage for VoLTE calls. Therefore, these (VoLTE) handsets are able to maintain longer conversations in comparison to CS (WCDMA) or OTT calls.

During a VoLTE call, subscribers may continue enjoying high-speed LTE data. What is more, data and voice services can cohabit in an efficient and seamless way based on the LTE radio interface design. Particularly, VoLTE offers a considerable network capacity as well as built-in QoS mechanisms, thus allowing for a reliable call quality irrespective of the large data traffic load.

4.1.2 Mobile Network Test: Testing Framework

For LTE subscribers to fully exploit the advantages the more advanced RF technology offers (including the data-intensive media services), a reliable network operational performance has to be ensured. This implies ongoing infrastructure inspections to timely identify and amend arising software and hardware issues.

---

[49] this is not the case for OTT services
[50] IMS, EPC, LTE with policy control

In the last few years, as the telecom sector has transitioned to HSPA and LTE technologies, the network intelligence has been increasingly 'relocated' from the core to the network's edge and then into the E-UTRAN Node B (eNB)[51]. In other words, a good deal of the control and decision making is currently implemented within the eNBs. For instance, the communication taking place among base stations (BS) and the UE can be best supervised by devices implicated in the particular transactions. For sure, one major driver (for the shift of the decision making entity involved in traffic management) is the latency demands for the sake of the LTE performance: the signaling control traffic must no longer pass through several network nodes when there is a modification for a UE.

Organizing a Drive Testing (DT)

The extensive performance assessment of a wireless network infrastructure (and its components) represents the fundamental goal of such a test. In fact, diverse settings like the availability level, call quality or the network coverage fall within the DT scope. Moreover, its execution appears meaningful after the installation of novel cell sites so as to make sure that these are properly incorporated into the network. Likewise, tests can be performed on a continuing basis to identify the root cause for a particular issue or to assess the network operational efficiency. Undeniably, the introduction of LTE has raised the significance of drive testing for MNOs.

Generally speaking, DT entails the data retrieval straight from a real network. The predefinition of several Key Performance Indicators (KPI) and their post-test verification would help analyze the QoS supplied by the network, thus analyzing the network performance from the subscriber's perspective. In this regard, potential problems like the frequency of dropped calls within a specific cell site (prior and after its upgrading) due to errors in the course of the implementation may be a good example for an issue a KPI need to address.

---

[51] also moving the traffic management toward the network boundary

Furthermore, DT is widely applied to supervise the handover[52] spot between legacy and LTE technologies. Particularly, the duration to conclude an originated handover, the data-interruption time (e.g. while moving among technologies) for the end-user and the success rates represent some KPIs that are carefully examined. Network optimization and benchmarking belong to the drive testing scope since they support MNOs in assessing the degree of (network) capacity utilization

Following resources are usually necessary during a DT:

- **Measuring device:** Typically, a minimum of two handsets will be employed: one is active (so as to perform call-based measurements), whereas the second device remains only attached to the network (e.g. inactive). Moreover, the call and idle mode performance can be assessed at different locations throughout the route.

  For instance, short and long calls are carried out to test diverse performance settings: long calls may provide an insight on handover characteristics, while short calls rather address signal-based features. Besides, the successful handover execution among contiguous cells can be determined based on speech quality, signal strength or download speed.

- **GPS system**: An illustration of the network coverage, including the likely areas of concern, can be generated based on the obtained test and GPS data.

- **Test vehicle**: This will be used to travel a specific route while obtaining test data. Obviously, the testing could also be performed on foot.

- **Computer comprising a data analysis/acquisition software**: Used for storage and (real-time) analysis of the data obtained.

---

[52] The signal quality, cell ID and neighbor information are evaluated before and after a handover for optimization purposes

4.2 Mobile Network Test 2014: Connect Magazine

As in previous years, the magazine 'Connect' assigned P3 communications with the realization of the network benchmarks. For this purpose, two measurement vehicles were deployed: each of them provided with ten[53] Samsung Galaxy S4 LTE+ handsets. Wherever applicable, the device's firmware[54] corresponded to the MNO's original one. Another test team, equipped with a portable measurement system, performed walk tests covering indoors and trains.

4.2.1 Organizational aspects

At the beginning of 2014, an initial meeting (P3 communications and Connect) took place to review the previous network test and outline the upcoming test framework: this comprised not only the test locations within the DACH[55] countries, but also a preliminary schedule based on the smartphones to be employed.

Based on the testing principles, each MNO's CTO[56] received comprehensive information concerning the testing logistics (e.g. services under test, locations, etc.) as well as the timetable. A feedback was then requested to prevent the test to be performed during a considerable network adjustment. In a later step, the presentation's official version including any comments on the test methodology was provided to the Technical Management.

Moreover, additional data provided to the MNO comprised the test outcomes prior to the final publication. Here, the aim was to offer adequate time to each MNO for the coming announcement of the test results. For the scoring and measurement methodology, Connect had at all times the final say.

---

[53] six to eight devices used for testing subject to the country
[54] Should no particular firmware be available, the up-to-date Samsung firmware was used
[55] Germany, Austria and Switzerland
[56] Chief Technology Officer

4.2.2 Test methodology

Throughout the measurements, two vehicles with predefined routes were in the same city, however not at the same location[57]. For static measurements, the vehicles halted at designated 'zones of interest' (train stations, airports or highly inhabited residential spaces). Interestingly, it was here where the measurement systems competed for the existing networks capacities with other subscribers.

In the case of Germany, the chosen locations were expected to account for a significant population share. Consequently, tests were performed in 21 large German cities while the smaller ones were travelled by one measurement vehicle on the way from one heavily populated city to the other. Furthermore, 16 densely populated cities were included in the case of Austria and Switzerland: In fact, around 20 small cities were also covered in each country. Similar to the German setting, highways were mostly travelled by the measurement vehicles.

---

[57] to avoid disturbances from one car to the other

Some basic points in terms of test methodology are described in Table 9.

Test Methodology	
Smartphone Data	Three main areas fell within the data test scope: data service capability, indoor coverage and download performance based on the (static) 'Kepler' test website[58]. In fact, using 3-4 Samsung handsets in the vehicles, many well-known websites were visited employing the integrated browser (sites were previously chosen according to the Alexa ranking[59]). For indoor or in-vehicle coverage, an offset of 12dB was introduced in the way from the antennas fixed on the vehicle's roof to the phones (in the car). Particularly, two antennas were used for each device since LTE applies the MIMO (Multiple Input Multiple Output) technology. Concerning the data service performance, upload and download files (1MB, 3MB) were sent from or to a test server. What is more, high definition videos (HD, 720p, 11.9MB, 30s) were streamed with the player provided by the phones.
Smartphone Telephony	For 2014, all MNOs in the DACH region offered LTE tariffs: all phones were hence preset to 'LTE preferred' mode and subject to CSFB after a call was initiated (previous to the call: attachment to a LTE cell). Basically, the tests on voice and data were performed using different handsets. For realistic conditions, data traffic was passing through the handsets for the duration of a call. Moreover, telephony was examined from one vehicle to the other (e.g. mobile-to-mobile). The obtained speech samples were then evaluated based on the POLQA algorithm.
Walk tests: in trains/indoors	For the walk tests, the procedure applied to data and voice services remained valid. This implied measurement spots while using the public transport or being around public buildings (including train stations, museums or airport terminals). Wherever possible, the test team travelled by train to other cities to assess the performance on the way to their destination.

Table 9: Network Test: Methodology

---

[58] as defined by ETSI for these testing scope
[59] A ranking system set by alexa.com (a subsidiary of amazon.com) that basically audits and makes public the frequency of visits on various Web sites.

4.2.3 Germany: Telephony Test Results

The German telecom sector in 2014 was not only characterized by considerable investments in LTE or fiber-optic networks, but also by takeovers (Kabel Deutschland by Vodafone) as well as mergers (E-Plus/Telefónica). Furthermore, the revenues in this German industry fell by 0,9%[60] to EUR 65 billion, which implies that the significant profit reduction derived from voice services could not be balanced by the (minor) growth in data services. Also, the earnings from mobile service decreased by approximately 1,6% to around EUR 19 billion (versus prior year's period). This can be understood as the result of the widely usage of IP services and social networks and, ultimately, to other MNO's aggressive pricing strategies. And despite these adverse developments, MNOs continue modernizing their networks. Some of the key findings for the voice services under test can be summarized as follows:

- The achieved success rates of Vodafone and Deutsche Telekom remained with 98,5% at a high level (refer to Table 10). For their part, E-Plus and O2 are left behind with rates near 96%
- Telekom, O2 and Vodafone possess a LTE share in the range 80%-90% in large cities, causing numerous CSFB handovers
- Concerning the drive test: outdoor measurements for Deutsche Telekom and Vodafone stayed at the same (good) level as the previous network test (a reliability enhancement of around 4,4% was even observed).
- The measurements on railways shed some negative light on the overall voice performance: E-Plus unsuccessful calls summed up to 21%, O2 and Telekom show only a slightly better ratio of 13% lost calls. For instance, around 3% of the calls carried some noise.
- In terms of CSFB performance, some HD voice parameters were missing generating a poor speech quality (the case of O2)

As stated in the first chapter, the numerical data throughout this paper uses a comma "," as decimal mark.

---

[60] according to an assessment of BITKOM (Federal Association for Information Technology, Telecommunications and New Media)

		Germany - Telephony Operators			
	Parameter	Deutsche Telekom	Vodafone	O2	E-Plus
TELEPHONY (BIG CITIES OUTDOOR)	Call Success Ratio (%)	98,5	98,5	95,7	96,0
	Call Setup Time (s)	6,3	6,3	9,1	6,3
	Speech Quality (MOS-LQO)	3,3	3,4	2,6	3,3
	Call Sustainability (%)	99,6	99,6	99,2	98,8
TELEPHONY (BIG CITIES INDOOR)	Call Success Ratio (%)	98,0	98,3	96,1	97,4
	Call Setup Time (s)	6,3	6,0	9,2	5,9
	Speech Quality (MOS-LQO)	3,4	3,4	2,6	3,4
	Call Sustainability (%)	99,7	99,6	99,8	98,7
TELEPHONY (HIGHWAYS)	Call Success Ratio (%)	97,6	95,4	93,1	92,5
	Call Setup Time (s)	7,1	7,1	10,2	6,9
	Speech Quality (MOS-LQO)	3,1	3,0	2,6	3,0
	Call Sustainability (%)	98,9	99,2	98,9	98,1
TELEPHONY (TRAINS)	Call Success Ratio (%)	86,7	83,9	85,5	78,6
	Call Setup Time (s)	7,6	7,3	9,7	8,0
	Speech Quality (MOS-LQO)	2,7	2,7	2,5	2,6
	Call Sustainability (%)	96,5	97,9	96,5	96,5

Table 10: Telephony (D): detailed test results according to operator and location. Adapted from [48]

4.2.4 Germany: Data Test Results

Indeed excellent service ratios for large cities and drive testing (better than 99% in almost all cases) were obtained. Particularly, Deutsche Telekom benefits from a satisfactory LTE coverage (1800 MHz). Some highlights are described below:

- The transfer/download speed, despite the rising traffic volume since the previous network test, witnessed a sound level especially for Deutsche Telekom (up to 40 Mbit/s and more than 11 Mbit/s in 90% of all measurements). Moreover, further indoor measurements attested the outdoor performance accurately.
- The upload tests (indoors) indicated, on the contrary, a slightly underperformance.
- A very good reliability was provided for the city outdoor setting. Streaming HD videos was successfully accomplished by most operators (E-Plus took the lead over O2 and Vodafone)
- Just one operator delivered poor results in regard to file retrieval and static internet surfing (E-Plus: 98,6% and 98,4% respectively).
- Adequate coverage was not always given for small towns: Vodafone ended up behind Telekom in terms of file transfer and internet surfing performance, which pointed to the reduced speed and reliability.

Germany - Data				
		Operators		
Parameter	Deutsche Telekom	Vodafone	O2	E-Plus
DATA (BIG CITIES OUTDOOR) WEB-PAGE DOWNLOAD (LIVE/STATIC)				
Success Ratio (%/%)	99,8 / 99,9	99,9 / 99,7	99,7 / 99,0	99,4 / 98,4
Avg. Session Time (s/s)	3,2 / 0,8	3,8 / 1,0	4,0 / 1,1	5,1 / 2,8
FILE-DOWNLOAD (3 MB)				
Success Ratio/Avg. Session Time (%/s)	99,8 / 1,6	99,8 / 2,5	99,9 / 2,6	98,6 / 4,5
90 % faster than (kbit/s)	11734	5475	5428	3340
YOUTUBE HD				
Success Ratio / Start Time (%/s)	99,5 / 0,9	98,7 / 1,4	98,9 / 1,5	96,8 / 2,1
Video playouts without interruptions (%)	98,9	97	98,2	94,3
DATA (BIG CITIES INDOOR) WEB-PAGE DOWNLOAD (LIVE/STATIC)				
Success Ratio (%/%)	99,4 / 99,6	99,4 / 99,7	99,2 / 99,5	98,9 / 98,8
Avg. Session Time (s/s)	3,5 / 0,8	4,4 / 1,1	5,3 / 1,3	5,5 / 1,7
FILE-DOWNLOAD (3 MB)				
Success Ratio/Avg. Session Time (%/s)	99,6 / 2,1	99,7 / 4,3	99,2 / 4,5	98,0 / 3,9
90 % faster than (kbit/s)	10729	4006	3023	3450
YOUTUBE HD				
Success Ratio / Start Time (%/s)	99,7 / 0,9	97,3 / 1,5	96,2 / 2,1	96,9 / 2,1
Video playouts without interruptions (%)	99,3	93,9	91,4	94,4
DATA (SMALL CITIES OUTDOOR) WEB-PAGE DOWNLOAD (LIVE/STATIC)				
Success Ratio (%/%)	99,6 / 99,7	98,9 / 96,8	98,6 / 98,0	99,3 / 97,8
Avg. Session Time (s/s)	3,4 / 0,9	4,6 / 1,9	5,5 / 2,2	6,1 / 3,3
FILE-DOWNLOAD (3 MB)				
Success Ratio/Avg. Session Time (%/s)	99,5 / 4,1	98,4 / 4,8	99,4 / 8,2	98,9 / 6,3
90 % faster than (kbit/s)	8386	2975	1956	2626
YOUTUBE HD				
Success Ratio / Start Time (%/s)	99,4 / 1,1	97,2 / 2,1	91,3 / 2,6	95,5 / 3,0
Video playouts without interruptions (%)	97,7	90,9	88,4	89,8
DATA ON HIGHWAYS WEB-PAGE DOWNLOAD (LIVE/STATIC)				
Success Ratio (%/%)	99,1 / 99,4	98,3 / 98,0	93,3 / 91,3	94,5 / 91,4
Avg. Session Time (s/s)	3,8 / 1,5	4,4 / 1,5	5,8 / 2,4	6,8 / 4,1
FILE-DOWNLOAD (3 MB)				
Success Ratio/Avg. Session Time (%/s)	98,4 / 3,5	98,2 / 4,6	91 / 12,2	92,1 / 13,1
90 % faster than (kbit/s)	5572	3836	269	593
YOUTUBE HD				
Success Ratio / Start Time (%/s)	98,1 / 1,4	96,1 / 1,8	94,6 / 2,1	89,9 / 3,1
Video playouts without interruptions (%)	96,8	92,4	91,8	85,1
DATA ON TRAINS WEB-PAGE DOWNLOAD (LIVE/STATIC)				
Success Ratio (%/%)	89,0 / 90,6	83,6 / 82,1	80,9 / 72,7	87,6 / 83,9
Avg. Session Time (s/s)	5,7 / 1,1	7,4 / 2,2	8,1 / 2,6	7,9 / 2,4
FILE-DOWNLOAD (3 MB)				
Success Ratio/Avg. Session Time (%/s)	86,1 / 7,1	72,8 / 18,9	61,9 / 23,9	77,6 / 12,8
90 % faster than (kbit/s)	320	111	100	144
YOUTUBE HD				
Success Ratio / Start Time (%/s)	93,4 / 1,4	87,5 / 3,6	90,2 / 4,4	85,3 / 4,0
Video playouts without interruptions (%)	92,7	76,8	74,4	78,9

Table 11: Data (D): detailed test results according to operator and location. Adapted from [48]

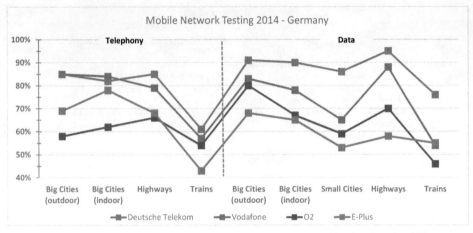

Figure 18: Germany: detailed test results according to operator and location. Based on [48]

4.2.5 Austria: Telephony Test Results

The telecom landscape in Austria is, with over 13 million SIM cards by the end of 2013, primarily concentrated on the mobile networks. The underlying data volume, which increased by 57% from 2012 to 2013, attests for the unbroken capacity development operators are expected to cope with. Furthermore, the solid (market) status demonstrated in past years is attributable the local MNO's high performance levels. Furthermore, some key factors identified in the network test 2014 are:

- For 2014, the achievement level of telephony in Austria remained at a high level. In other words, high performing German operators represent a baseline for Austrian counterparts
- T-Mobile and Drei succeeded in deploying LTE, which is translated in success ratios in the range 98,4%-98,7% in cities. These results were clearly surpassed by A1 Telekom Austria and Drei
- In terms of stability on the highways among cities: A1 Telekom Austria and Drei accomplished, despite the slightly decrease in performance, success ratios around 97%-98%, followed by T-Mobile with 95%

Austria - Telephony Operators			
Parameter	A1 Telekom Austria	T-Mobile	Drei
TELEPHONY (BIG CITIES OUTDOOR/INDOOR) Call Success Ratio (%)	98,7 / 99,1	98,4 / 98,7	98,7 / 99,8
Call Setup Time (s)	5,7 / 6	5,7 / 5,6	6,8 / 6,9
Speech Quality (MOS-LQO)	3,6 / 3,7	3,5 / 3,6	3,7 / 3,8
Call Sustainability (%)	99,9 / 99,7	99,6 / 99,7	99,8 / 99,7
TELEPHONY (HIGHWAYS/TRAINS) Call Success Ratio (%)	97,9 / 90,8	95,0 / 85,9	97,1 / 82,6
Call Setup Time (s)	5,7 / 5,5	6,5 / 6,3	7,4 / 7,7
Speech Quality (MOS-LQO)	3,6 / 3,4	3,3 / 3,2	3,5 / 3,4
Call Sustainability (%)	99,5 / 98,7	99,4 / 98,7	99,6 / 98,5

Table 12: Telephony (A): detailed test results according to operator and location. Adapted from [48]

4.2.6 Austria: Data Test Results

Data services entails, for many operators, a (market) differentiation potential. As a result, impressive success ratios (better than 99,5%[61]) were realized in large cities for uploads/downloads as well as web surfing. In the same manner, MNOs showed a similar development in small cities: T-Mobile and Drei are trailing A1 Telekom Austria in terms of performance (even if reliability is moderately higher for T-Mobile and Drei). Some of the key findings can be summarized as follows:

- For A1, the average download speed advanced from 13 Mbit/s to 52 Mbit/s[62]. This improvement is, however, not reflected when surfing in the web: the loading time of 2.2 seconds for A1 is just 0,8 seconds faster than for the two other MNOs
- The average data rates for Drei improved, based on 2013 figures, from 7 Mbit/s to 30 Mbit/s
- The data performance on trains showed a clear ranking winner (A1), followed by Drei and T-Mobile. Moreover, the case of highways resemble to that of cities, with Drei closing the gap to A1's performance and outperforming T-Mobile.

---

[61] only for YouTube HD two MNO surpassed the 99% threshold due to the marginally rise of interruptions
[62] this is associated with the (YouTube) HD service offered by A1

Austria - Data			
		Operators	
Parameter	**A1 Telekom Austria**	**T-Mobile**	**Drei**
DATA (BIG CITIES OUTDOOR)			
WEB-PAGE DOWNLOAD (LIVE/STATIC)			
Success Ratio (%/%)	99,7 / 99,6	99,8 / 99,7	99,8 / 99,5
Avg. Session Time (s/s)	2,2 / 0,6	2,8 / 1,2	3,0 / 1,6
FILE-DOWNLOAD (3 MB / 1 MB)			
Success Ratio/Avg. Session Time (%/s)	99,5 / 99,7	99,9 / 99,8	99,5 / 99,5
90 % faster than (kbit/s)	2355 / 4379	7397 / 1136	4419 / 1207
YOUTUBE HD			
Success Ratio / Start Time (%/s)	99,9 / 100	99,8 / 98,6	99,8 / 99
Video playouts without interruptions (%)	99,9 / 99,8	99,6 / 97,8	99,7 / 97,1
DATA (BIG CITIES INDOOR)			
WEB-PAGE DOWNLOAD (LIVE/STATIC)			
Success Ratio (%/%)	99,7 / 99,8	99,7 / 99,4	99,8 / 100
Avg. Session Time (s/s)	2,5 / 0,6	2,8 / 0,7	3,8 / 1,5
FILE-DOWNLOAD (3 MB / 1 MB)			
Success Ratio/Avg. Session Time (%/s)	99,8 / 99,8	99,8 / 99,6	99,2 / 100
90 % faster than (kbit/s)	2132 / 2782	11452 / 1159	3266 / 634
YOUTUBE HD			
Success Ratio / Start Time (%/s)	100 / 99,8	99,8 / 98,8	99,6 / 96,0
Video playouts without interruptions (%)	100 / 99,6	99,8 / 98,6	99,2 / 91,8
DATA (SMALL CITIES OUTDOOR)			
WEB-PAGE DOWNLOAD (LIVE/STATIC)			
Success Ratio (%/%)	97,9 / 96,9	99,0 / 97,7	99,8 / 99,6
Avg. Session Time (s/s)	3,0 / 1,8	3,7 / 2,0	3,7 / 2,2
FILE-DOWNLOAD (3 MB / 1 MB)			
Success Ratio/Avg. Session Time (%/s)	99,2 / 98,4	100 / 99,2	98,5 / 99,3
90 % faster than (kbit/s)	1085 / 890	5063 / 667	2421 / 1239
YOUTUBE HD			
Success Ratio / Start Time (%/s)	100 / 98,4	98,4 / 98,4	100 / 94,6
Video playouts without interruptions (%)	100 / 97,6	98,4 / 97,6	100 / 90,0
DATA ON HIGHWAYS			
WEB-PAGE DOWNLOAD (LIVE/STATIC)			
Success Ratio (%/%)	97,7 / 97,3	98,0 / 96,5	98,9 / 98,4
Avg. Session Time (s/s)	3,4 / 2,2	4,8 / 3,2	4,2 / 2,8
FILE-DOWNLOAD (3 MB / 1 MB)			
Success Ratio/Avg. Session Time (%/s)	97,5 / 98,8	97,8 / 99,1	98,0 / 99,1
90 % faster than (kbit/s)	841 / 530	1207 / 318	2482 / 863
YOUTUBE HD			
Success Ratio / Start Time (%/s)	99,1 / 98,3	97,1 / 94,5	98,4 / 96,1
Video playouts without interruptions (%)	98,9 / 98,1	96,4 / 93,3	97,3 / 93,9
DATA ON TRAINS			
WEB-PAGE DOWNLOAD (LIVE/STATIC)			
Success Ratio (%/%)	96,1 / 96,4	96,5 / 96,9	96,8 / 97,8
Avg. Session Time (s/s)	4,1 / 1,8	5,5 / 2,5	6,2 / 3,0
FILE-DOWNLOAD (3 MB / 1 MB)			
Success Ratio/Avg. Session Time (%/s)	91,4 / 95,8	95,3 / 98,4	91,6 / 97,2
90 % faster than (kbit/s)	392 / 301	763 / 317	827 / 195
YOUTUBE HD			
Success Ratio / Start Time (%/s)	98,3 / 94,6	93,9 / 84,1	97,1 / 80,7
Video playouts without interruptions (%)	97,8 / 90,4	91,7 / 81,8	91,9 / 69,3

Table 13: Data (A): detailed test results according to operator and location. Adapted from [48]

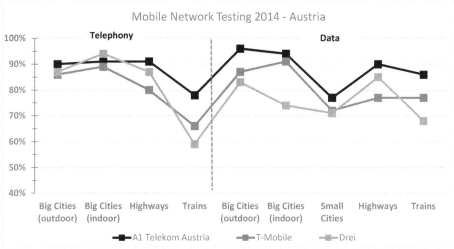

Figure 19: Austria: detailed test results according to operator and location. Based on [48]

4.2.7 Switzerland: Telephony Test Results

The Swiss telecom market, having three operators by the end of 2014, is characterized by a wide range of voice/data services as well as its innovative spirit. For instance, the increasing merging of IT, telecommunications and media is shaping the market, thus attracting additional global players. For their part, these novel contestants are providing cost-effective Internet-based services like SMS messaging, telephony or TV. In this regard, cloud-based approaches are becoming sort of 'game changers' (e.g. more relevant) as processing power, storage capacity, etc. tend to progressively migrate to the Internet.

As a result of the high market penetration, the growth of SIM cards ownership (0,8% by the end of 2014) was for a consecutive time sluggish. Particularly, the (achievement) gap railways versus highways became evident again in spite of the exceptionally high railway usage in this country. Some highlights are described below:

- All three MNOs achieved success ratios in the range of 99% (telephony)
- In terms of call setup time, Sunrise outperformed (despite the similarity of the high LTE share) all other MNOs with 4,4 – 4,5 seconds. As for speech quality, Sunrise and Swisscom attained good MOS levels (3,4 – 3,5), tightly followed by Orange

- As for reliability on the highways among cities, the achieved level for all MNOs stayed indeed high. Likewise, the calls quality on trains was remarkably good (Orange being the top performer in this category).

	Switzerland - Telephony Operators		
Parameter	Swisscom	Sunrise	Orange
TELEPHONY (BIG CITIES OUTDOOR/INDOOR) Call Success Ratio (%)	98,6 / 99,4	98,9 / 99,4	98,4 / 99,6
Call Setup Time (s)	7,5 / 7,2	4,5 / 4,4	5,9 / 5,8
Speech Quality (MOS-LQO)	3,4 / 3,5	3,4 / 3,5	3,2 / 3,4
Call Sustainability (%)	99,7 / 99,5	99,4 / 99,8	99,5 / 99,9
TELEPHONY (HIGHWAYS/TRAINS) Call Success Ratio (%)	97,8 / 93,7	97,7 / 91,6	97,2 / 96,5
Call Setup Time (s)	7,5 / 7,9	4,6 / 4,9	5,8 / 5,9
Speech Quality (MOS-LQO)	3,4 / 3,3	3,3 / 3,2	3,1 / 3,1
Call Sustainability (%)	99,7 / 98,8	98,8 / 97,2	99,6 / 99,5

Table 14:Telephony (CH): detailed test results according to operator and location. Adapted from [48]

4.2.8 Switzerland: Data Test Results

In fact, average speeds showed an enhancement of more than 50% compared to 2014, leading to almost perfectly retrieved YouTube videos. This can be translated in average upload speeds of 27Mbit/s and 35Mbit/s for downloads (Swisscom). Or in other words: retrieving a web site did last 3 seconds at maximum.

- Success ratios of 99%-100% for mobile Internet in cities are common for all MNOs
- The (reliability) performance on trains and highways ended up slightly behind the 100% mark. For YouTube HD, this gap was marginally higher (especially for Orange).

Switzerland - Data			
		Operators	
Parameter	Swisscom	Sunrise	Orange
WEB-PAGE DOWNLOAD (LIVE/STATIC)			
Success Ratio (%/%)	99,4 / 99,6	99,5 / 99,6	99,4 / 99,2
Avg. Session Time (s/s)	2,7 / 1,1	2,6 / 1,1	3,0 / 1,1
DATA (BIG CITIES OUTDOOR) FILE-DOWNLOAD (3 MB / 1 MB)			
Success Ratio/Avg. Session Time (%/s)	99,8 / 99,9	99,8 / 99,8	99,5 / 99,9
90 % faster than (kbit/s)	11619 / 4613	4908 / 1871	7221 / 2497
YOUTUBE HD			
Success Ratio / Start Time (%/s)	99,9 / 99,3	99,7 / 98,7	99,8 / 99,0
Video playouts without interruptions (%)	99,8 / 98,9	99,5 / 97,3	99,7 / 98,4
WEB-PAGE DOWNLOAD (LIVE/STATIC)			
Success Ratio (%/%)	99,5 / 100	99,5 / 99,8	99,6 / 100
Avg. Session Time (s/s)	2,8 / 0,9	2,6 / 1,0	3,0 / 0,9
DATA (BIG CITIES INDOOR) FILE-DOWNLOAD (3 MB / 1 MB)			
Success Ratio/Avg. Session Time (%/s)	99,8 / 99,7	99,8 / 99,5	99,8 / 100
90 % faster than (kbit/s)	10774 / 3023	8742 / 2700	10150 / 3963
YOUTUBE HD			
Success Ratio / Start Time (%/s)	100 / 99,8	100 / 99,3	100 / 99,8
Video playouts without interruptions (%)	100 / 99,8	100 / 99,3	100 / 99,6
WEB-PAGE DOWNLOAD (LIVE/STATIC)			
Success Ratio (%/%)	99,9 / 100	99,8 / 99,7	99,9 / 99,7
Avg. Session Time (s/s)	2,7 / 1,1	2,7 / 1,4	2,9 / 1,1
DATA (SMALL CITIES OUTDOOR) FILE-DOWNLOAD (3 MB / 1 MB)			
Success Ratio/Avg. Session Time (%/s)	100 / 100	100 / 100	100 / 100
90 % faster than (kbit/s)	13296 / 6182	4286 / 1399	6289 / 1254
YOUTUBE HD			
Success Ratio / Start Time (%/s)	100 / 100	100 / 96,1	100 / 99,3
Video playouts without interruptions (%)	100 / 98,7	100 / 94,8	100 / 98,0
WEB-PAGE DOWNLOAD (LIVE/STATIC)			
Success Ratio (%/%)	99,1 / 98,9	98,7 / 99,3	97,9 / 96,3
Avg. Session Time (s/s)	3,1 / 1,6	3,2 / 1,9	3,6 / 1,8
DATA ON HIGHWAYS FILE-DOWNLOAD (3 MB / 1 MB)			
Success Ratio/Avg. Session Time (%/s)	99,3 / 99,5	98,0 / 99,0	96,8 / 97,4
90 % faster than (kbit/s)	6379 / 2059	2535 / 1094	2537 / 1376
YOUTUBE HD			
Success Ratio / Start Time (%/s)	99,7 / 98,2	98,8 / 96,1	99,1 / 96,2
Video playouts without interruptions (%)	99,7 / 97,2	98,2 / 94,2	98,8 / 95,4
WEB-PAGE DOWNLOAD (LIVE/STATIC)			
Success Ratio (%/%)	98,2 / 98,1	97,9 / 98,0	97,6 / 98,0
Avg. Session Time (s/s)	3,8 / 1,3	4,4 / 1,9	4,0 / 1,5
DATA ON TRAINS FILE-DOWNLOAD (3 MB / 1 MB)			
Success Ratio/Avg. Session Time (%/s)	98,6 / 97,6	95,6 / 96,6	97,0 / 99,0
90 % faster than (kbit/s)	2685 / 692	1622 / 928	2352 / 1165
YOUTUBE HD			
Success Ratio / Start Time (%/s)	98,5 / 96,4	97,0 / 89,3	98,0 / 96,4
Video playouts without interruptions (%)	98,5 / 93,8	95,5 / 82,7	97,5 / 93,8

Table 15: Data (CH): detailed test results according to operator and location. Adapted from [48]

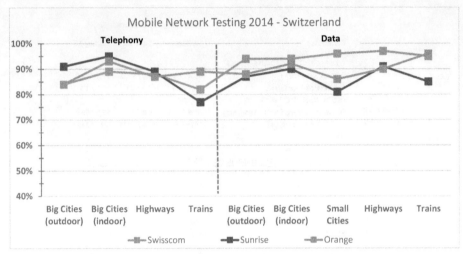

Figure 20: Switzerland: detailed test results according to operator and location. Based on [48]

4.2.9 Mobile Network Test: Overall Results DACH Region

Undeniably, providing fast LTE speeds combined with reliable voice (2G/3G) involves, as exposed by the last mobile network benchmark, a balancing act for each MNO. Taking the top performing Swiss operator (Swisscom) as a reference point, it is clearly demonstrated how the room for development could be best capitalized. Swisscom[63] offered even in rural areas an excellent coverage level.

In Austria, the performance benchmark is definitely given by A1 Telekom Austria with its high-speed and wide-ranging data network. With regard to (high quality) speech transmission, A1 Telekom Austria also outperformed other competitors. Nevertheless, a network performance improvement was observed for T-Mobile: from 13 Mbit/s to 28 Mbit/s soared the download throughput[64]. By contrast, T-Mobile's some weaker points comprised HD videos and data uploads in small cities or telephony on railways. Drei's data services were likewise negatively rated during the test.

---

[63] with 60% market share
[64] average within the past 12 months (previous to the network test)

Last but not least, the German Deutsche Telekom (local test winner) was able to provide high quality telephony[65] services in large and less populated cities. In addition, O2 showed some voice quality weaknesses owing to its recent LTE deployment. For the merged Telefónica/E-Plus, the upcoming network test should show a progress in terms of LTE coverage and ultimately of their data service level. Vodafone shone, for its part, with fast and reliable data services.

Table 16 shows the summarized results for the network benchmark in the DACH region.

		DACH Region - Operators									
		Germany				Austria			Switzerland		
		Deutsche Telekom	Vodafone	O2	E-Plus	A1 Telekom Austria	T-Mobile	Drei	Swisscom	Sunrise	Orange
Telephony	max. 210	175	171	128	145	188	175	183	181	189	182
Big Cities (outdoor)	95	85%	85%	58%	69%	90%	86%	87%	84%	91%	84%
Big Cities (indoor)	35	82%	84%	62%	78%	91%	89%	94%	89%	95%	93%
Highways	70	85%	79%	66%	68%	91%	80%	87%	88%	89%	87%
Trains	10	61%	57%	54%	43%	78%	66%	59%	82%	77%	89%
Data	max. 290	261	229	207	182	265	242	230	275	253	259
Big Cities (outdoor)	135	91%	83%	80%	68%	96%	87%	83%	94%	87%	88%
Big Cities (indoor)	50	90%	78%	67%	65%	94%	91%	74%	94%	90%	92%
Small Cities	35	86%	65%	59%	53%	77%	72%	71%	96%	81%	86%
Highways	50	95%	88%	70%	58%	90%	77%	85%	97%	91%	90%
Trains	20	76%	54%	46%	55%	86%	77%	68%	95%	85%	96%
Rating	max. 500	436	400	335	327	453	417	413	456	442	441
connect		very good	good	satisfactory	satisfactory	very good	good	good	very good	very good	very good

Table 16: DACH Region: Telephony and Data test results by operator. Adapted from [48]

4.2.10   Austria: VoLTE Friendly User Tests

Some operators[66] across the DACH region participated during 2014 in Friendly User Tests (FUT): this assessment was, however, limited to specific (country) regions activated for VoLTE measurements. In fact, the MNOs provided also the smartphones used for the measurements (equipped with their own VoLTE firmware).

As shown in the anonymized Table 17, the failure rates for four network operators were extremely low. The two remaining ones have major (E) or minor (A) issues to solve before seriously thinking of implementing VoLTE. If the connections with at least a handover to the 3G network are considered, the success rate for three operators reached the 99%

---

[65] this strong performance was also observed on rural routes despite some weaknesses in trains
[66] Deutsche Telekom, Vodafone, E-Plus, O2, Swisscom and A1 Telekom Austria

mark. Moreover, the short call setup time are noticeable with 2 to maximum 4 seconds on average (with precondition). Though, a source of debate may be given by the 0,5 seconds (call setup time) achieved by operator D.

In addition, P3 communications has examined the latency in voice transmissions[67]: three operators achieved below 150 milliseconds, whereas the rest touched the limit of approximately 200 milliseconds (a range required for an undisturbed conversation).

Concerning voice quality, the accomplished MOS value (3,3 - 3,9) improved by 0,8 points compared to the test average for 2013. This significant progress proves VoLTE as a suitable standard in terms of reliability and quality. Remarkably, VoLTE cannot only support additional call partners within a radio cell, but also (thanks to the all-IP approach) makes the core network cost-effective for operators.

Anonymized VoLTE call statistics DACH Operators						
Parameter	A	B	C	D	E	F
Call Success Ratio (%)	95,8	100,0	99,3	99,4	87,6	100,0
Call Setup Time (s)	2,0	2,1	2,1	2,1	3,7	1,9
Call Setup Time min./max.(s)	0,8/10,5	1,0/5,5	0,6/4,7	0,5/6,0	2,5/19,1	1,1/5,7
Speech Quality (MOS-LQO)	3,5	3,8	3,6	3,8	3,3	3,9

Table 17: First VoLTE call statistics DACH Region 09/2014. Adapted from [49]

4.3 Mobile Network Test 2014: CHIP Magazine

The network test 2014 of the magazine 'CHIP' focused solely on four German operators. The test engineers of NET CHECK, CHIP's test partner, covered some 5.600 kilometers (one third of the time by car, public transport and on foot respectively) and collected more than 100.000 individual measurements. For the most densely populated cities in each state, the testers assigned enough time to allow for detailed measurements.

---

[67] defined as the time required for words to be heard by the opposite party

The evaluation scheme emphasized the mobile data access (60%) over telephony (40%). Furthermore, different modules for telephony and data access performance were defined: measurements along the highways were weighted with 10% and those along the state roads and public metropolitan/suburban railway with 25% each. The remaining 40% were equally assigned to measurements within the main traffic arteries and those obtained while walking.

4.3.1 Test methodology

Two measuring systems consisting of twelve operational smartphones were employed: four Galaxy S3 LTE were dedicated to test the telephony, other four S3 LTE retrieved permanently videos from YouTube and four Samsung Galaxy S5 were testing the performance when uploading/downloading large amounts of data. Also, the Galaxy S5 already support LTE Category 4 with multiple antenna systems (MIMO), allowing theoretical data rates of up to 150 Mbit/s.

The test vehicle travelled throughout German highways and rural roads, driving them on secondary routes through sparsely populated areas. While driving, the equipment comprised two measuring systems (QualiPoc Free Rider II), each having 6 smartphones. The smartphones were kept in a specially designed box on the car roof. No vehicle-mounted external antennas were used as in 2013. Instead, the internal antennas of smartphones were used to test the multi-antenna MIMO technology under realistic conditions.

While using the public transport, the measuring systems were moved from the roof box into two special backpacks. The testers then walked into the inner cities and travelled among the main traffic arteries of each city to guarantee the widest possible test coverage.

4.3.2 Germany: Telephony Test Results

For the assessment of mobile networks, calls (to the smartphones) were initiated from fixed line networks as well as from the mobile devices themselves. A successful call setup was planned to last around two minutes, in which several speech samples were exchanged between the smartphone and the measurement computer (at the other end). The underlying speech sample was automatically evaluated based on the POLQA algorithm.

As a rule of thumb, samples showing a MOS value below 2,7 can cause serious problems in understanding the other party. The evaluation scheme for voice quality involves, therefore, the success rate (25%), call setup time (10%), call stability (25%) and the quantity of 'poor' speech samples (40%) with a MOS score below 2,7.

	Parameter	Germany - Telephony			
		Operators			
		Deutsche Telekom	Vodafone	O2	E-Plus
TELEPHONY (HIGHWAYS)	Call Success Ratio (%)	97,8	95,7	96,9	98,0
	Interrupted Calls (%)	0,0	1,0	3,0	3,3
	Call Setup Time (s)	7,0	7,6	8,0	6,5
	Share Poor Speech Samples - MOS below 2,7 (%)	4,9	4,6	8,9	6,5
TELEPHONY (COUNTRY ROADS)	Call Success Ratio (%)	98,3	95,9	96,6	96,6
	Interrupted Calls (%)	1,0	1,8	1,7	1,7
	Call Setup Time (s)	6,8	7,3	7,7	6,6
	Share Poor Speech Samples - MOS below 2,7 (%)	4,0	4,4	5,1	7,6
CITIES (BY CAR)	Call Success Ratio (%)	98,5	98,9	97,0	98,9
	Interrupted Calls (%)	0,3	0,3	0,3	1,1
	Call Setup Time (s)	6,7	7,6	8,7	7,5
	Share Poor Speech Samples - MOS below 2,7 (%)	2,5	2,4	4,0	5,4
CITIES (BY PUBLIC TRANSPORT)	Call Success Ratio (%)	97,9	97,2	97,5	97,6
	Interrupted Calls (%)	2,0	2,4	1,8	2,4
	Call Setup Time (s)	6,7	7,5	8,2	7,1
	Share Poor Speech Samples - MOS below 2,7 (%)	2,7	2,7	4,7	3,4
CITIES (ON FOOT)	Call Success Ratio (%)	98,4	98,0	97,7	97,2
	Interrupted Calls (%)	0,0	0,0	0,5	0,2
	Call Setup Time (s)	7,0	7,6	8,7	7,3
	Share Poor Speech Samples - MOS below 2,7 (%)	2,2	1,5	3,5	1,4

Table 18: Telephony (D): detailed test results according to location. Adapted from [20]

4.3.3 Germany: Data Test Results

As stated above, eight smartphones[68] were dedicated to evaluate the mobile data access (download/upload rates), streaming of YouTube videos and web browsing. The predefined weighting ratios represented 60% for web browsing, 25% for data throughput and 15% for video streaming.

Moreover, the evaluation of the data throughput foresaw additional (performance) factors like the maximum retrieved data within 30 seconds: the success rate accounted for 50%, the average data throughput over the measuring time (25%) and the percentage of data connections having a data throughput above 2 Mbit/s (upload) or 5 Mbit/s (download) were weighted with 25% as well.

Besides, the reliability of web browsing was likewise severe evaluated: in case a test website could not be completely displayed after 30 seconds, the test case was graded unsuccessful. In this case, 50% of the points were assigned based on the success rate, the remaining 50% awarded for the fastest possible website load. A similar approach applied to streaming (YouTube) videos: 40% of the points were awarded for a successfully streamed media file. Another 40% for brief interruptions and the last 20% were granted for the shortest possible initial delay.

---

[68] four Samsung Galaxy S5 and four Samsung Galaxy S3 LTE were used in parallel

		Germany - Data			
			Operators		
	Parameter	Deutsche Telekom	Vodafone	O2	E-Plus
DATA (HIGHWAYS)	Download Success Ratio (%)	99,1	93,0	87,0	92,0
	Average Download Rate (Mbit/s)	21,3	13,6	10,8	8,2
	Upload Success Ratio (%)	99,4	94,9	88,9	89,2
	Average Upload Rate (Mbit/s)	9,9	10,4	5,4	2,5
	Success Ratio Website retrieval (%)	95,7	93,7	76,7	85,4
	Duration Website retrieval (s)	5,4	5,1	7,8	8,4
	Success Ratio retrieved Youtube videos (%)	96,3	80,4	46,2	62,4
DATA (COUNTRY ROADS)	Download Success Ratio (%)	98,3	94,3	88,8	85,9
	Average Download Rate (Mbit/s)	24,3	12,7	10,8	11,3
	Upload Success Ratio (%)	98,3	93,3	87,0	85,7
	Average Upload Rate (Mbit/s)	13,7	8,9	6,3	4,1
	Success Ratio Website retrieval (%)	94,6	90,8	82,0	81,4
	Duration Website retrieval (s)	5,7	6,3	6,9	7,8
	Success Ratio retrieved Youtube videos (%)	87,8	80,9	54,5	60,9
CITIES (BY CAR)	Download Success Ratio (%)	99,0	95,9	99,0	98,0
	Average Download Rate (Mbit/s)	37,3	17,5	13,6	14,7
	Upload Success Ratio (%)	99,1	96,3	97,0	99,3
	Average Upload Rate (Mbit/s)	25,0	13,6	9,2	6,3
	Success Ratio Website retrieval (%)	98,6	98,5	97,5	97,7
	Duration Website retrieval (s)	4,3	4,5	5,7	6,4
	Success Ratio retrieved Youtube videos (%)	99,6	98,6	92,4	95,0
CITIES (BY PUBLIC TRANSPORT)	Download Success Ratio (%)	96,4	93,9	95,1	94,1
	Average Download Rate (Mbit/s)	27,3	13,2	12,2	12,7
	Upload Success Ratio (%)	96,0	93,3	93,4	93,4
	Average Upload Rate (Mbit/s)	14,4	9,2	6,2	4,2
	Success Ratio Website retrieval (%)	94,5	94,3	93,4	92,6
	Duration Website retrieval (s)	5,3	5,2	6,3	6,9
	Success Ratio retrieved Youtube videos (%)	95,3	86,3	89,9	83,4
CITIES (ON FOOT)	Download Success Ratio (%)	99,8	94,6	99,3	99,3
	Average Download Rate (Mbit/s)	33,1	18,1	14,2	15,9
	Upload Success Ratio (%)	100,0	95,8	97,7	99,3
	Average Upload Rate (Mbit/s)	22,9	13,3	9,1	6,5
	Success Ratio Website retrieval (%)	99,1	98,2	98,2	97,4
	Duration Website retrieval (s)	4,3	4,3	5,4	6,2
	Success Ratio retrieved Youtube videos (%)	99,6	94,7	97,7	90,9

Table 19: Data (D): detailed test results according to location. Adapted from [20]

5 Conclusion

According to [30] [47], the global ICT market rose by 4% in 2014. Particularly, this was the result of the solid demand for telecom services and facilities, mainly in the USA and Asia. Another highlight in the previous year was given by the strong (telecom) industry's consolidation pressure in Europe, triggered by dropping returns [30]. In the end, the decisive objective of further investing in network roll-outs is to effectively deal with the escalating data speed/volume requirements. Fortunately, MNOs are successfully showing their capabilities in coping with these challenges. And this benefits not only subscribers or the telecom sector, but also fosters a self-governing digital economy.

In this sense, VoLTE may boost a MNO's network productivity and further enrich the subscriber's experience in terms of call setup times and speech quality. Consequently, VoLTE embodies the MNO's imminent strategy and progress towards novel communication services this industry must deal with. For instance, it is not a matter of deciding whether to implement VoLTE or not, but instead of selecting the proper tactical approach to do it. In this sense, IMS's cost-effectiveness and flexibility as well as its capability to provide for IP services (regardless of the access method) enabled it to become the favorite approach for delivering core services within an all-IP setting.

Furthermore, major efforts should be undertaken to deal with events threatening a first-class voice experience, e.g. being outside LTE coverage (prior to a conversation) or quitting the LTE coverage range after a call origination. This scenario is indeed relevant since extensive LTE coverage, throughout the initial LTE deployments, cannot be assumed.

Meanwhile, IP communications are being accepted as the next evolutionary step of core mobile services. Operators are, therefore, called to continue investing in their networks (e.g. IP infrastructure) so as to enjoy a superior brand positioning and be able to 'switch-off' their legacy networks in the medium term[69]. Additionally, greater control over supplementary access methods (Wi-Fi for example) as well as an increased need for MNO's core applications is the VoLTE promise in the long run.

---

[69] Or at least include legacy networks in an ICS architecture

Forthcoming challenges

The network test 2015 focused on new features like LTE Advanced along with Carrier Aggregation (CA), (super) wideband voice connections as well as VoLTE measurements [49]. A1 Telekom Austria successfully assessed its telephony service over LTE (VoLTE trial) in the second quarter 2014, following the implementation of LTE CA in certain Austrian cities by the end of 2014 (speeds of up to 300 Mbps were achieved with proper devices). There is, however, a long way to go in view of the well-equipped and motivated market players in the DACH region (Swisscom for instance).

Interoperability poses, in addition, a challenge when it comes to fully realize the inherent potential of IP communications. In fact, the extent to which operators support interconnection (and roaming to some degree) will decide on the MNO's ability to exploit the benefits coupled with IP communications.

Looking ahead

Despite some deployment issues or extensive consensus, the telecom sector gives a good impression of being prepared for IP-communications. In this regard, the 'journey' away from industry-driven towards to demand driven growth is expected as a direct consequence of the emergent acceptance of HD calling and VoLTE in the subscriber's mind [30]. Undoubtedly, VoLTE is gradually being perceived as a premium device's in-built feature, likely to be found already 'in the box'.

Finally, no matter where competitive pressures or regulation initiatives of technology enhancements might take the telecom business within the next few years, MNO's (financial) endeavors in favor of VoLTE will enable them to handle in a forward-looking and customer-friendly way.

Bibliography

[1]   3GPP, The Evolved Packet Core, available on http://www.3gpp.org/technologies/keywords-acronyms/100-the-evolved-packet-core [last access on 01.02.2015]

[2]   3GPP, TR 23.856, Single Radio Voice Call Continuity (SR-VCC) enhancements; Stage 2., available on http://www.3gpp.org/ftp/Specs/html-info/23856.htm [last access on 01.03.2015]

[3]   3GPP. TS 22.278, Service requirements for the Evolved Packet System (EPS), available on http://www.3gpp.org/ftp/Specs/html-info/22278.htm [last access on 01.03.2015]

[4]   3GPP. TS 23.216, Single Radio Voice Call Continuity; Stage 2, available on http://www.3gpp.org/ftp/Specs/html-info/23216.htm [last access on 01.03.2015]

[5]   3GPP. TS 23.237, IP Multimedia Subsystem (IMS) Service Continuity; Stage 2, available on http://www.3gpp.org/ftp/Specs/html-info/23237.htm [last access on 01.03.2015]

[6]   3GPP. TS 23.401, General Packet Radio Service (GPRS) enhancements for Evolved Universal Terrestrial Radio Access Network (eUTRAN) access, available on http://www.3gpp.org/ftp/Specs/html-info/23401.htm [last access on 01.03.2015]

[7]   3GPP, TS 24.237, IP Multimedia (IM) Core Network (CN) subsystem IP Multimedia Subsystem (IMS) service continuity; Stage 3, available on http://www.3gpp.org/ftp/Specs/html-info/24237.htm [last access on 01.03.2015]

[8]   3GPP, TS 25.304, User Equipment (UE) procedures in idle mode and procedures for cell reselection in connected mode, available on http://www.3gpp.org/ftp/Specs/html-info/25304.htm [last access on 01.03.2015]

[9]   3GPP. TS 22.173, IP Multimedia Core Network Subsystem (IMS) Multimedia Telephony Service and supplementary services; Stage 1, available on http://www.3gpp.org/DynaReport/22173.htm [last access on 01.03.2015]

[10]   3GPP, TS 23.292: IP Multimedia Subsystem (IMS) centralized services; Stage 2, available on http://www.3gpp.org/DynaReport/23292.htm [last access on 01.03.2015]

[11]   3GPP, TS 24.008: Mobile radio interface Layer 3 specification; Core network protocols; Stage 3, available on http://www.3gpp.org/dynareport/24008.htm [last access on 01.03.2015]

[12]   3GPP TS 23.228: IP Multimedia Subsystem (IMS); Stage 2, available on http://www.3gpp.org/DynaReport/23228.htm [last access on 01.03.2015]

[13]   4G Americas, VoLTE and RCS Technology Evolution & Ecosystem, 2014

[14]   Alcatel-Lucent, Options for Providing Voice over LTE and Their Impact on the GSM/UMTS Network, Strategic White Paper, 2009

[15]   Alcatel-Lucent, Service Consistency for Today's VoLTE Subscribers, Technology White Paper, 2011

[16]   Alcatel-Lucent, Voice over LTE: The new mobile voice, Strategic White Paper, 2012

[17]   Alcatel-Lucent, Service Continuity for Today's VoLTE Subscribers, Technology White Paper, 2012

[18]   A. Perez, Voice over LTE: EPS and IMS Networks, John Wiley & Sons, First Edition, 2013

[19]   Audio   Precision,   PESQ   and   POLQA   Options,   available   on http://www.ap.com/products/apx/perceptual [last access on 14.02.2015]

[20]   CHIP Digital, Netztest 2014, available on http://www.chip.de/artikel/Der-haerteste-Handy-Netztest-Deutschlands-Telekom-Vodafone-O2-und-E-Plus-im-Test_63944005.html   [last access on 01.03.2015]

[21]   Cisco, Voice over Long Term Evolution Migration Strategies, White Paper, 2012

[22]   Deutsche Telekom, Annual Report 2014, available on https://www.telekom.com/ar-2014 [last access on 10.04.2015]

[23]   European Commission, Digital Agenda for Europe, Europe 2020 Strategy, available on https://ec.europa.eu/digital-agenda/our-goals/pillar-i-digital-single-market [last access on 10.04.2015]

[24]   Ericsson, Evolved HD voice for LTE, White Paper, 2014

[25]   Ericsson,   Mobility   Report   2014,   available   on http://www.ericsson.com/res/docs/2014/ericsson-mobility-report-november-2014.pdf   [last access on 19.03.2015]

[26]   Ericsson, Mobility Report. Mobile World Congress Edition, available on http://www.ericsson.com/res/docs/2015/ericsson-mobility-report-feb-2015-interim.pdf   [last access on 25.03.2015]

[27]   Ericsson, Validating voice over LTE end-to-end, Ericsson Review, 2012

[28]   Ericsson, Voice and video calling over LTE, White Paper, 2014

[29]   GSMA, IMS Profile for Voice and SMS, Official Document IR.92, 2014

[30]   GSMA,   The   Mobile   Economy   2015,   available   on http://www.gsmamobileeconomy.com/GSMA_Global_Mobile_Economy_Report_2015.pdf [last access on 02.04.2015]

[31]   GSMA, VoLTE Service Description and Implementation Guidelines, Official Document FCM.01, 2014

[32]   Huawei, Full HD Voice, White Paper, 2014

[33]   J. Rankin, A. Costaiche, J. Zeto, Validating VoLTE - A Definitive Guide to Successful Deployments, First Edition, CreateSpace Independent Publishing Platform, 2013

[34]   M. Poikselkä, H. Holma, J. Hongisto, J. Kallio, A. Toskala, Voice over LTE (VoLTE), John Wiley & Sons, First Edition, 2012

[35]   Nokia Networks, Evolve to richer voice with Voice over LTE (VoLTE), White Paper, 2014

[36]   Nokia Networks, Voice over LTE (VoLTE) Optimization, White Paper, 2014

[37]   POLQA Coalition, POLQA Technology, available on http://polqa.info/index.html [last access on 15.02.2015]

[38]   Qualcomm, VoLTE with SRVCC: The second phase of voice evolution for mobile LTE devices, White Paper, 2012

[39]   Rohde & Schwarz, Next-Generation (3G/4G) Voice Quality Testing with POLQA, White Paper, 2012

[40]   Rohde & Schwarz, IOT & VoLTE, R&S IOT/PQA Seminar, available on http://www.digitimes.com.tw/tw/b2b/seminar/service/download/053a111160/053a111160_ku 4os9wcy1p3lzfl8trd.pdf [last access on 25.02.2015]

[41]   Signals Research Group, Behind the VoLTE curtain (Part 1), Vol. 10, Number 7 PREVIEW, 2014

[42]   Signals Research Group, Behind the VoLTE curtain (Part 2), 2015

[43]   Spirent, IMS Architecture. The LTE User Equipment Perspective, White Paper, 2014

[44]   Spirent, VoLTE Deployment and the Radio Access Network. The LTE User Equipment Perspective, White Paper, 2012

[45]   Swisscom, Annual Report 2014, available on https://www.swisscom.ch/en/about/investors/reports.html [last access on 15.04.2015]

[46]   Telecoms.com Intelligence, VoLTE: Why, When and How?, White Paper, 2013

[47]   Telekom Austria, Annual Report 2014, available on http://www.telekomaustria.com/en/ir/annual-reports [last access on 09.04.2015]

[48]   Weka Media Publishing, Connect Netztest 2014/2015, available on http://http://www.connect.de/netztest/ [last access on 01.03.2015]

[49]   Weka Media Publishing, Anruf der vierten Generation, Connect Magazine 12/2014, pages 70-74

List of Figures

List of Tables

List of Abbreviations

2G	Second generation
3G	Third generation
3GPP	3rd Generation Partnership Project
AAA	Authentication, Authorization and Accounting
ACR	Anonymous Call Rejection
AMBR	Aggregate Maximum Bit Rate
AMR	Adaptive Multi-Rate
AMR-WB	Adaptive Multi-Rate Wideband
API	Application Programming Interface
APN	Access Point Name
ARP	Allocation and Retention Priority
ARPU	Average Revenue Per User
AS	Application Server
A-SBC	Access Session Border Controller
AUTN	Authentication Token
AVP	Attribute Value Pair
AWS	Advanced Wireless Spectrum
BGCF	Border Gateway Control Function
BICC	Bearer Independent Call Control
BSC	Base Station Controller
BSS	Base Station System
CAMEL	Customized Applications for Mobile network Enhanced Logic
CDIV	Communication Diversion
CDMA	Code Division Multiple Access
CN	Core Network
CONF	Conferencing
CS	Circuit Switched
CS NAS	Circuit Switched Non-Access Signaling
CSCF	Call Session Control Function
CSFB	Circuit Switched Fall Back
CW	Call Waiting
DEA	Diameter Edge Agent
DiffServ	Differentiated Services
DL	DownLink
DNS	Domain Name System
DPI	Deep Packet Inspection
DRA	Diameter Relay Agent
DRX	Discontinuous Reception
DTM	Dual Transfer Mode
ECGI	E-UTRAN Cell Global Identifier
EDGE	Enhanced Data rates for GSM Evolution
eNode B	Evolved Node B

EPC	Evolved Packet Core
EPS	Evolved Packet System
ERAB	E-UTRAN Radio Access Bearer
ESM	EPS Session Management
eSRVCC	Enhanced Single Radio Voice Call Continuity
ETSI	European Telecommunications Standards Institute
E-UTRAN	Evolved UTRAN
E-UTRAN	Evolved Universal Terrestrial Access Network
FDD	Frequency Division Duplex
G3	Fax Group 3 Fax
GAA	Generic Authentication Architecture
GA-CSR	Generic Access - Circuit-Switched Resources
GAN	Generic Access Network
GBA	Generic Bootstrapping Architecture
GBR	Guaranteed Bit Rate
GERAN	GSM EDGE Radio Access Network
GGSN	Gateway GPRS Support Node
GPRS	General Packet Radio Service
GSM	Global System for Mobile Communications
GSMA	GSM Association
GTP	GPRS Tunneling Protocol
HLR	Home Location Register
HPMN	Home Public Mobile Network
HSPA	High Speed Packet Access
HSPA+	Evolved High Speed Packet Access
HSS	Home Subscriber Server
HTTP	Hypertext Transfer Protocol
IBCF	Interconnection Border Control Function
ICS	IMS Centralized Services
I-CSCF	Interrogating Call Session Control Function
ICSI	IMS Communication Service Identifier
IETF	Internet Engineering Task Force
iFC	Initial Filter Criteria
IMEI	International Mobile Equipment Identity
IM-GW	IP Media Gateway
IMS	IP Multimedia Subsystem
IMS-AGW	IMS Access Gateway
IMS-AKA	IMS Authentication and Key Agreement
IMS-ALG	IMS Application Level Gateway
IMSI	International Mobile Subscriber Identity
IOT	Interoperability Testing
IP	Internet Protocol
IP-CAN	IP-Connectivity Access Network
IPsec	IP Security

IP-SM-GW	IP Short Message Gateway
IPX	IP Packet Exchange
I-SBC	Interconnect Session Border Controller
ISC	IMS Service Continuity
ISIM	IM Services Identity Module
ISUP	ISDN User Part
IWF	Interworking Function
LTE	Long Term Evolution
MAC	Medium Access Control
MBR	Maximum Bit Rate
MCC	Mobile Country Code
ME	Mobile Equipment
MGCF	Media Gateway Control Function
MGW	Media Gateway
MIMO	multiple-input multiple-output
MME	Mobility Management Entity
MMS	Multimedia Messaging Service
MMTel	Multimedia Telephony
MNC	Mobile Network Code
MNO	Mobile Network Operator
MOS	Mean Opinion Score
MRF	Media Resource Function
MSC	Mobile Switching Center
MSISDN	Mobile Subscriber ISDN Number
MSRP	Message Session Relay Protocol
MTU	Maximum Transmission Unit
MWI	Message Waiting Indicator
NAPTR	Name Authority Pointer
NAS	Non-Access Stratum
NAT	Network Address Translation
NNI	Network to Network Interface
OIP	Originating Identification Presentation
OIR	Originating Identification Restriction
OSS	Operations Support System
OTT	Over-The-Top
PCC	Policy and Charging Control
PCEF	Policy and Charging Enforcement Function
PCO	Protocol Configuration Options
PCRF	Policy Charging and Rules Function
P-CSCF	Proxy Call Session Control Function
PDN	Packet Data Network
PDN-GW	PDN Gateway
PLMN	Public Land Mobile Network
PS	Packet Switched

PSHO	PS handover
QCI	QoS Class Identifier
QoS	Quality of Service
RAB	Radio Access Bearer
RAN	Radio Access Network
RAND	RANDom number (used for authentication)
RAT	Radio Access Technology
RCS	Rich Communication Suite
RES	user RESponse (used in IMS-AKA)
RLC	Radio Link Control
RNC	Radio Network Controller
RNS	Radio Network Subsystem
ROHC	Robust Header Compression
RRC	Radio Resource Control
RTCP	RTP Control Protocol
RTP	Real-time Transport Protocol
SAE	System Architecture Evolution
SBC	Session Border Controller
SCC AS	Service Centralization and Continuity Application Server
S-CSCF	Serving - Call Session Control Function
SCTP	Stream Control Transmission Protocol
SDP	Session Description Protocol
SEG	Security Gateway
SGSN	Serving GPRS Support Node
SGW	Serving Gateway
SIGCOMP	Signalling Compression
SIP	Session Initiation Protocol
SMS	Short Message Service
SPD	Speech Path Delay
SRVCC	Single Radio Voice Call Continuity
TAI	Tracking Area ID
TAS	Telephony Application Server
TCP	Transmission Control Protocol
UE	user equipment
UMA	Unlicensed Mobile Access
UMTS	Universal Mobile Telecommunications System
UTRAN	UMTS Terrestrial Radio Access Network
VANC	VoLGA Access Network Controller
VoIP	Voice over IP
VoLGA	Voice over LTE via Generic Access